Heavy Music Mothers

EXTREME SOUNDS STUDIES: GLOBAL SOCIO-CULTURAL EXPLORATIONS

Series Editors: Niall Scott, Nelson Varas-Díaz, and Bryan Bardine

Music and sound do not take place in a social vacuum. They manifest themselves, and are a reflection of, particular social contexts. They are grounded in geographies, people's lived experiences, and specific events. Therefore, when we conceptualize music and sound as "extreme," we do so in recognition of this contextual anchoring, and as an acknowledgment that contexts are both <u>produced</u>, and <u>reflected</u>, through them. Metal music studies have used the terminology of "extreme music" to describe sounds, aesthetics, and practices that are usually interpreted as distant from, and challenging of, the societies in which music is created and consumed.

This book series aims to explore how the idea of "the extreme" might serve to understand the roles of sounds in our lives. It aims to address the following questions: What makes some kinds of music and sounds extreme? Is there an aesthetic of extreme in music and sound to be unpacked that can be encountered elsewhere, for example in the analysis of noise or other forms of experimental music, even in the extremity of the mundane? How do diverse people and communities think about the extreme when referencing music and sound? In other words, it is not always clear what the term extreme refers to, and yet it is all around us. This book series aims to fill this gap.

Recent Titles

Heavy Music Mothers: Extreme Identities, Narrative Disruptions, by Julie Turley and Joan Jocson-Singh

Defiant Sounds: Heavy Metal Music in the Global South, edited by Nelson Varas-Díaz, Jeremy Wallach, Esther Clinton, and Daniel Nevárez-Araújo

Music, Sound, and Documentary Film in the Global South, edited by Christopher L. Ballengee

Heavy Music Mothers

Extreme Identities, Narrative Disruptions

Julie Turley and Joan Jocson-Singh

LEXINGTON BOOKS
Lanham • Boulder • New York • London

Rowman & Littlefield
Bloomsbury Publishing Inc, 1359 Broadway, New York, NY 10018, USA
Bloomsbury Publishing Plc, 50 Bedford Square, London, WC1B 3DP, UK
Bloomsbury Publishing Ireland, 29 Earlsfort Terrace, Dublin 2, D02 AY28, Ireland
www.bloomsbury.com

Published by Lexington Books
An imprint of The Rowman & Littlefield Publishing Group, Inc.
4501 Forbes Boulevard, Suite 200, Lanham, Maryland 20706
www.rowman.com

86-90 Paul Street, London EC2A 4NE

Copyright © 2023 by The Rowman & Littlefield Publishing Group, Inc.

All rights reserved. No part of this publication may be: i) reproduced or transmitted in any form, electronic or mechanical, including photocopying, recording or by means of any information storage or retrieval system without prior permission in writing from the publishers; or ii) used or reproduced in any way for the training, development or operation of artificial intelligence (AI) technologies, including generative AI technologies. The rights holders expressly reserve this publication from the text and data mining exception as per Article 4(3) of the Digital Single Market Directive (EU) 2019/790.

British Library Cataloguing in Publication Information available

Library of Congress Cataloging-in-Publication Data

Names: Turley, Julie, author. | Jocson-Singh, Joan, author.
Title: Heavy music mothers: extreme identities, narrative disruptions / Julie Turley and Joan Jocson-Singh.
Description: Lanham: Lexington Books, 2023. | Series: Extreme sounds studies: global socio-cultural explorations | Includes bibliographical references and index.
Identifiers: LCCN 2023002606 (print) | LCCN 2023002607 (ebook) |
  ISBN 9781666916157 (cloth) | ISBN 9781666916164 (ebook)
Subjects: LCSH: Women rock musicians. | Mothers. | Motherhood—Social aspects. | Heavy metal (Music)—Social aspects.
Classification: LCC ML82 .T865 2023 (print) | LCC ML82 (ebook) |
  DDC 781.66092/52—dc23/eng/20230203
LC record available at https:// lccn.loc .gov/2023002606
LC ebook record available at https:// lccn.loc.gov/2023002607

Contents

Acknowledgments	vii
Introduction	ix
Chapter 1: Mother Framing	1
Chapter 2: The Stories We Tell	9
Chapter 3: The Rock Mom Memoir	55
Chapter 4: Vigilante Motherhood: The Embrace of Anger	79
Chapter 5: Daughters on Rock Moms: Life, Performance, Musicking, and Bonding	85
Chapter 6: Mother Tracks: Rock and Metal Moms Write Motherhood	95
Conclusion	109
References	115
Index	121
About the Authors	129

Acknowledgments

It goes without saying that our biggest *thanks* goes to all the mothers who participated in our research: in loose alphabetical order, Alexandre, Annie, Mallika, Nicole, Helixx C. Armageddon, Kari Auerbach, Christy Davis of Slowness et al., Emily Duff of the Emily Duff Band, Dana Marie Embree, Tanya Hockley, Jessica Hopper of *Women Who Rock* et al., Darryl LaVare, Nancy Maloney, Moan Elisa of the Trash Bags, Dafna Naphtali, Puma of Puma Perl and Friends, Cynthia Ross of the 'B' Girls et al., Sara Whizbanger of *The Whizbanger Show*, Dana Schwister of No Fun, Julie Unruly of High & Tight, and Mary Zadroga of Jane Lee Hooker. This book gets its power chords from their generosity, thoughtfulness, and willingness to share essential stories. These were busy, hustling mothers who gave generously of their already limited time, whether it was in person, via Zoom, or through email correspondence. Such insights and stories of 'lived' experiences are the rock 'n' roll heart of this book. In addition, the radical and rich stories we've collected here have taught us that motherhood, and musicking motherhood in particular, remains a challenge not only in life, but in the still male-dominated music industry.

Julie would like to extend a special horns-up to singer-songwriter Amy Rigby, whose brilliant memoir *Girl to City* was not only invaluable to more than one chapter in this book, but who took the time to respond personally to Julie's inquiries and dig up and send along footage of a 1990 performance of The Shams.

Further, and on a very personal note, Joan would like to dedicate completing this project to her very good friend and mother, Julia Jin, who passed away right as this project started. Without her encouragement and exuberant personality, persevering with such an endeavor seemed almost insurmountable.

Last, but not least, Joan and Julie could not have undertaken this project in such a personal and profound way without the presence of their own daughters. It was these daughters, four in total, who inspired this project and continue to make their respective mothers' worlds meaningful and complex: they made Julie and Joan the mothers they are and continue to teach them about joy, necessary rough edges, patience, and yes, music! *Thank you, Stella, Zoë, Ella, and Kara. Rock on!*

Introduction

> After giving birth, I told the doctor I needed to leave the hospital for five hours. Our band was opening for Johnny Thunders. I think I was on an adrenaline rush.
>
> Cynthia, 67, 'B' Girls/Renegades/New York Junk

Motherhood. Tough, rewarding, painful, brutal as a metal music track, and as exhilarating as The Runaways' "Cherry Bomb." Sometimes it's as exhilarating as giving birth, as referenced by Cynthia Ross above. Thinking of how to describe the various identities and roles we take up as mothers in our everyday lives while working, being a wife, a partner, a friend, and a sole autonomous self from all the conventions placed on "good" versus "bad" mothering—is as thoroughly exhausting as it sounds. What does motherhood mean anyway? There are many who "mother," who are in caregiving roles, but who don't occupy that structural slot. How does one decide what defines a mothering moment to describe those very important moments that make up motherhood? And how *are* important moments defined? Can it be defined on stage—away from children? Or with children in the wings of a stage? How, as mothers who musick, can we process the conflict between creative liminality and the cultural ideology of motherhood? Do we have to? And who are the women who have been voicing this experience? Or who is now articulating it through our book? Much of the research for this book has been compiled here to give voice to the very mothers who have long wrestled with and have answered these questions. The result of this research takes a variety of forms—as vignettes with firsthand accounts giving insight to what those experiences are like and why our male counterparts aren't asked the same questions. Flipping back to the indices of books on "women and music," "music and feminism," "the gender of rock," and scanning the "M" sections for "mother," or "motherhood" has foregrounded to us how much of a void exists on the topic of music and mothering; scanning indices has been a largely fruitless activity. Why is the experience of mothering so often missing from these books that focus on rock and metal music women? The mother gaps in music studies, we feel, is egregious. We also started this motherhood study for personal reasons, outlined in the ethnographic portion of our book.

Musicking, a term first coined by professor-musician Christopher Small (Small 1990) is the active way in which we all take part in the creation of music and in establishing relationships with society—musicking then is considered a form of active engagement and meaning-making, whether we're dancing to music, singing along to the radio, or creating music in our bedrooms or on stage. This study recognizes much of what exists at the intersection of motherhood and musicking. There is an abundance of scholarly literature on mothers who emotionally, financially, and logistically support their "musicking" children. Indeed, the concept of "musicking children" has become something of a ubiquitous signifier of "successful" and albeit, high intensity mothering. Against this context, this study vigorously responds to the fact that there is a dearth of literature on mothers who themselves "musick," and whose music participation decenters children—or attempts to—within the intensive mothering model.

No matter where women are in terms of gender equality, motherhood has been and will continue to be a visceral and all-encompassing experience, at times even traumatic. One moment humbling and quiet, and then—boom—dynamic and bombastic. And the global pandemic seems to have made these extremes even more extreme. Pondering the extremes of motherhood, it won't come as a surprise to any mother that there's nothing more extremely "metal" than giving birth, the inexorable changes to the body and mind. The relentlessness of taking care of an infant and beyond. As mothers, we're both inside and outside this body, afflicted with a self-imposed alienation that places us in a liminal space of outsideness, or rather insideness that is othered; a "grotesque realism" Bakhtin claims ([1936] 1984,19), that equally offers liberation and catharsis of the mundane in motherhood.

This book starts from a place of critical self-reflection. In examining the idiosyncratic motherhood identity at the core of this book, we start with our own stories, how we ourselves hurtled into motherhood and developed our own respective "mother" identities.

JOAN'S STORY

My earliest memories of music and my own mother were road trips to the Catskills as a child. Taking the long drive upstate, meandering through farms that my city friends rarely saw, an occasional red barn on the side of the road, like something out of a picture book. It was always fall when we headed up

Introduction xi

Figure I.1. Joan Jocson-Singh and daughters, Ella and Kara.
Source: Photo by Joan Jocson-Singh

north and so our path was a kaleidoscope of bright orange and red leaves with the sun peeking through. My mother loved the Supremes and Elvis, and so our car was filled with tunes that inevitably influenced my love for sweet tambourine and bass-driven sounds: moving beats that were easy for my seven-year-old body to dance to. When I think back about the importance of music, that Supremes song, "I Hear a Symphony," echoes in my brain and cements moments that can only be seen along this very song—images of my mother and father smiling while arguing which stop to get gas for the car, my brother reading a Stephen King novel as we travel along the highway, and seeing the '80s-era vinyl peel-and-stick tint off my side window with the views of sunshine and trees. It wouldn't be until much later, when I myself became a mother, that I would realize how the very idea of parenting, and motherhood in particular, can be a unique vehicle for embodying and conveying its own creative space. For me, I found reinvention and solace in metal music; for Julie, it was punk.

Nothing could soothe me more than the indecipherable sounds heard from someone like Karyn Crisis—her vocals often alternating from clean to guttural screams as she takes up space to reinvent both mother and womanhood. Her latest band—Gospel of the Witches—and their song "Mother"—created just the right interstitial space in which I could find catharsis. Much of death and doom metal has been this for me. The deep tonalities and aggressive blast-beats, so often gendered as masculine attributes, spoke to my emotional and transgressive experience of mothering. My listening experience in extreme metal transcended me. It offered me a space of resistance to my conventional life. My waking and professional life was where I was always "on"—as a mother, as a wife, and as a librarian. Many of our interviewees echoed this need to have a space separate from their identities as mothers. Spaces that allowed them to rage, to resist, and to breathe.

I came into my relationship with metal late, as my first loves were '80s new wave, that is, Joy Division, OMD, Depeche Mode, the Cure, and punk bands like the Clash, Swingin' Utters, and Minor Threat. I was very much a throwback new waver swimming in a sea of '90s pop, "alternative" rock, and hip hop from my early junior high school days up until my last year of high school when I started listening to punk. I blame it on having a sister eleven years older than me who often left vinyl records lying around the house with covers that could do nothing but fascinate my thirteen-year-old self.

Growing up in Yonkers, a suburb of New York City, life was, at times, surprisingly nondiverse. In my mind, it has always been the City's sixth borough, and with New York City's reputedly sheer abundance of artistic variety, it was surprising to me that while growing up there, I could not find others with the same interest in the music that I gravitated toward. Sure, my peers were predominantly Hispanic, Latino, Black, and Asian kids, but in terms of musical diversity, my environment fell victim to the typical genre that preteens and teens listened to: popular music. During the '90s, while teens in my school were listening to Britney Spears, NSYNC, or Boys II Men, I was listening to the Cure and OMD. Because of my dated taste in music, I wasn't part of the in-crowd. I found solace in hanging out with my older siblings like the dweeby little sister in one of those John Hughes movies, anxiously trying to see what cool things my brother and sister were doing. When they threw parties, I was soaking up the subculture. It was no wonder when I look back, I didn't have the same interests as other teens my age. I was simply thirteen going on twenty-four. My love of new wave transitioned into a love of metal as I found certain new wave bands carried the same rhythmic heaviness that I would later find in metal. Joy Division's heavy bass lines, accompanied by Ian Curtis's haunting and despairing baritone voice, transformed over time into the doom and death metal that I came to enjoy. Lyrically, Joy Division penned songs about death, life, and the human condition, themes that I would also encounter in much of the death metal I later heard.

In the early 2000s, I remember listening to Metallica's self-titled album and thinking it was the heaviest thing I had ever heard. As a teen, nothing could compare to both the heaviness and the lyrical poetry vocalized by James Hetfield in "The Unforgiven" or "Nothing Else Matters." I felt an even greater sense of connection reading about Kirk Hammett being half-Filipino. There I was, a young Filipina, feeling validated that a half-Filipino guy could rock lead guitar in such a quintessential band! I didn't care what his other half was.

But it was years later, in 2005, when my relationship with metal—particularly death and doom metal—*truly deepened*. As time progressed, so did my transition to listening to heavier and heavier strains of metal. Unlike the average adolescent white male metalhead of the time who listened to more mainstream metal like Korn, Slipknot, or System of a Down, I started listening to extreme metal music (EMM) in my mid-twenties, not gravitating towards it due to any coming-of-age or rebellious stage of teenage-hood (Arnett 1996), but rather because of a life change. My mother died when I was twenty-three. All of a sudden, the deep tonalities that I could find only within EMM rose to fill a void that no other music could. The deep growling vocals and aggressive blast-beats of death metal provided a form of transgressive and emotional experience for me. Being that the majority of bands are male-dominated in EMM, finding women musicians and vocalists that embodied the volume of rage and anger I felt was extremely rewarding. I found this catharsis listening to Karyn Crisis (Crisis) and Dawn Crosby (Fear of God). When I was eighteen and first heard death metal, I had the same knee-jerk reaction that most people who are unfamiliar with extreme music have, which was, "What is this shit?!" I still vividly remember when my then boyfriend played Carcass for me for the first time. It was a song from their album *Heartwork*, and I remember telling him what he had just played for me was "not music." At the time, my ears couldn't process the unfamiliar signature changes, the frenetic pace, and even the hyper-shrieked vocal elements. With time, I listened and became familiar with it. As I aged and my life transitioned from feelings of grief and death to hopefulness, my appreciation for EMM deepened. Whatever the reason Carcass didn't speak to my eighteen-year-old self, the band snarled into my CD tray at twenty-five. *Heartwork* has since become one of my favorite death metal albums for its energy and intensity. What resonated was that although EMM was known for having misogynistic and aggressive lyrics, the content ranged from not just death, gore, and alienation, but also to social commentaries on art, politics, philosophy, and the human condition (Kahn-Harris 2007, 10–11; Purcell 2003, 188). *Heartwork*, in particular, cloaked these explications in medical terminology and thesaurus-fueled wordplay that took repeated listening to truly appreciate, and which over time grew more meaningful. Although controversial with fans for its transitional status from grindcore to metal, *Heartwork* proved to be a gateway to what intellectual, poetic and non-misogynistic metal could be while retaining the key sonic elements that identified it as extreme metal. However, for all my love of the sound, the image of the metalhead as portrayed in popular culture was not one that I identified with. I am not a man, white, preteen, or deviant (Arnett 1996, 7; Walser 1993, 109–10; Weinstein 1991, 66). I came to realize that the lack of women role models in extreme metal is still an issue today. Whereas the general metal music subculture has seen the roles of women increase with five notable figures like Doro Pesch (Warlock), Lita Ford and Joan Jett (Runaways), and related acts like Sean Yseult (White Zombie) and Amy Lee (Evanescence), the media often only highlights women vocalists of mainstream heavy metal. Women in the EMM scene, like Jo Bench (Bolt Thrower), Angela Gossow (Arch Enemy), and Karyn Crisis (Crisis, Gospel of the Witches) remained relatively underground in comparison. When you add motherhood as a parameter, the representation gets even smaller.

Back in 2012, I hardly knew any other pregnant mothers who were listening to Chuck Shuldiner's album *Human* and finding inspiration to finish their thesis work, or attending Napalm Death shows, six months pregnant. Death's *Human* would give me additional insight into how metal could be a space away from misogyny through their poetic and dystopian songs about politics and the human condition. Such social commentary in musical format resonated with my ideas of feminism. There I was, an Asian American woman, going to metal shows in New York with her then Trinidadian American husband, where the demographics, even in a diverse borough like Manhattan, was still heavily scaled toward white men. I recall being one of the few Asian women in most metal music audiences. Adding the intersection of my ethnicity to the picture often lent itself to a duality of how one performs and engages within the metal music scene. Am I fetishized as a woman, an Asian woman, a pregnant woman? Are their subcultural coded behaviors that I was supposed to adhere to? Where was I represented in the music that I consumed? Is there an assumption that I am submissive, shouldn't like metal music, or not expose my very own daughters to the same music?

As far as BIPOC women, myself and my fellow Black women friends were often the smallest demographic after white and Hispanic women. Data and narratives we've gathered from the mothers in our study validates this. Overwhelmingly, the women included here and from our online survey identified as white, female, and cis-hetero. Where possible, in our vignettes, we've included women who identify as BIPOC. Yet such a small sample offers insight to how each musical genre are still problematic spaces regarding ethnicity and those who participate, gender withstanding. Julie and I acknowledge this privilege and positionality and continue to find ways to increase more visibility of BIPOC women and non-binary identifying people who musick and mother.

Our book aims to give power to the stories and assumptions that identification and involvement in these musical subcultures, traditionally hostile to women and profoundly incongruous to motherhood, is essential to these mothers' practice of self-care and empowerment.

So why here and why now? What's the story we're telling? For me, I claim another life change, one that was gradual and unexpected. It's working full-time, having gone to graduate school, losing one of my best friends, becoming a mother and watching my twenty-year-long marriage deteriorate. At the heels of the circular way we can handle grief, I went to the first place that ever felt like home—*music*. Ironically, it is my soon-to-be ex who introduced me to metal and it's where I've once again found solace. Like any typical story where separation occurs, I had high hopes to keep alive a friendship and healthy co-parenting relationship. But the inability of that relationship to thrive pushed me to see how as mothers, the emotional and even visible labor can get dismissed over years. I had felt alone in the rearing of my two girls, and because I was young when this relationship with my ex had blossomed, I hadn't been equipped with the communication tools needed to question why I had normalized our unhealthy codependency. The most surprising thing that arose from this study for me was that many other women resonated with this dismissal. And they too found solace, and even empowerment through music. That's what this book gives voice to—the collective women of rock and metal sharing their experiences of motherhood and music.

JULIE'S STORY

Figure I.2. Julie Turley and daughters, Zoë and Stella, 2010.
Source: Photo by Darryl LaVare

My story pushes off legendary English rock mom Marianne Faithfull's, particularly a moment from her life detailed in Tanya Pearson's lucid and ingenious 2021 biography *Why Marianne Faithfull Matters*. By age nineteen, mother of a baby, Marianne "bored, trapped, and exhausted [. . .] partied and wandered around London, returning to the apartment every four hours to breastfeed, a physical manifestation of her internal conflict, one experienced by many women who felt shortchanged by the promises of marriage and motherhood at a time when it seemed like the world was opening up" (Pearson 2021, 48). Marianne in 1966 was like a young Mormon mom in 1986, sans heroin and Andrew Loog Oldham. In the Mormon experience, in many ways, it's always 1966 for women. By the time I had my first kid at age thirty-four, I thought it was too late for me. I did not anticipate boredom. I yearned to be a mom. In Mormon time, it had taken me forever to get married. By the time I was almost thirty-one, my Mormon family had pretty much given up on me. For me, a white cis-gendered female born into a fifth-generation Mormon family, motherhood was an expectation and imperative, a "divine role," part and parcel of the highest degree of eternal glory in Mormon theology. The only way out of it in this life was infertility or remaining single and childless. But for young Mormon women of my generation, upper Gen Xers, refusal was not an option. In Mormonism, refusing marriage and motherhood meant you were willfully impeding the eternal progression of spirit children, *your* children in waiting, the ones who had chosen *you,* whose body they needed in order to descend to earth to begin their own "eternal progression." This entire plan is sketched in the iconic Mormon pop cultural "text" The Osmond Brothers' 1973 album *The Plan.* And before the smash hit *The Book of Mormon* on Broadway, the quasi-rock musical *Saturday's Warrior*, performed in Mormon church cultural halls all over the United States in the '70s and '80s, and became a feature film in 2016. This musical references the faith's most bombastic heavy metal scenario, that Mormon women have the potential to be goddesses—Mothers in Heaven, hair blown back by some cosmic winds, ruling, along with their God husbands, over planets full of children. Uber motherhood. But it was my own very mortal mother who troubled this Mormon ideal: my mother found this "divine role" so challenging, she tried to ignore it, as well as the four earthly children she often seemed surprised to have. For her, self-care consisted of collapsing on the couch in front of the daytime TV programming in our southern Arizona tract home, or escaping out the door with car keys to make a grocery run by herself. In the span of time her children were at school, she wrote of her depression in spiral bound notebooks stacked under the TV stand. My mother's 2012 autism diagnosis explained much—her version of a beleaguered Erma Bombeckian motherhood was one without the irony or the laughs—and made it possible, years later, for her children, ensconced in their own parenting roles, to feel some compassion, while slowly unpacking what transpired from years of a mother's neglect. Granted, my mother's generation, the women who gave birth in the '60s and '70s, are not characterized as practitioners of a child-centric intensive mothering. My most vivid childhood memories are of free-range wanderings: extracting once a surreally large lightbulb from the neighbors' trash and biking home one handed with it, loitering in front of an open vat of battery acid, peeing outside, drinking from random rusty garden hoses, discussing Elton John's creepy "Someone Saved My Life Tonight" on the playground as I pulled up my knee socks.

    I picked up rock music via complaint. My devout Mormon father, a junior high school teacher, spoke grimly of the junior high school acid rock of the dances he endured as a chaperone. Anything that I would later come to know as culturally vital and interesting—*Jesus Christ Superstar*, the Equal Rights Amendment, feminism—my parents dismissed with fear and derision. Maybe it's a key characteristic of '70s kids left to pick through a cultural mess of things that leaked out or landed by accident like lightbulbs from the garbage:

incidental music from TV programming, musical guests on *Saturday Night Live* that I had to sneak out and watch, covering the television set with a blanket. In a bedroom, a small stack of albums, soundtracks of iconic musicals from my mother's girlhood, but nothing to play them on. And in adolescence, the palm-size Radio Shack radio—a sonic campfire—my sister and I huddled around in the church parking lot: Casey Kasem finishing up the *Top 40* countdown before we had to put the radio away and go inside to take the sacrament. With my parents, I did not quite feel safe enough to explore rock music as an identity, as a mode to express . . . what? I wasn't sure exactly. Between my mother's emotional absence and my father's employment precarity, it felt like the height of selfishness to be aberrational, to make Jesus cry, to come home with a mohawk, or even pierced ears. I followed all the rules and waited. I sang hymns with my fellow Mormons in endless sacrament meetings. I was in the Mormon show choir, called—what else?—The Mormonairs. Since the presidency and "reign" of Brigham Young, Mormons had been encouraged to use music as a vehicle for worship and praise. It was not cool, but I sang my Mormon music loudly. As with most high demand religions, music functioned as a tool of propaganda, to keep us in line, facilitating a singleness of intent on our divine roles, apart from trouble, away from anything resembling boundary-crossing blues.

Keeping track of tracks that punctuate my portion of this introduction, one can't help but note the preponderance of male rockers. My musical memory is full of them: from eight-year-old me writing ardent fan mail to David Cassidy to seventeen-year-old me ruminating on the hotness of Rick Springfield on MTV. My senior year of high school, the entire graduating class, except for the Latinx lowrider kids with their Earth, Wind & Fire, seemed to listen to Rush and Pink Floyd. Car stereos blasted either REO Speedwagon or AC/DC. Loverboy's "The Kid is Hot Tonight" made our winning routine tight at summer cheerleading camp.

Ironically, it was on the main campus of Mormon college—Brigham Young University in Provo, Utah where I was made aware of rock, classic rock, punk rock, new wave. It turns out there were "cool Mormons," riding into town with boom boxes and cassette tapes on Vespas and retro mod parkas from Huntington Beach, Burbank, San Diego, San Clemente, Las Vegas— the places Brigham Young sent weary converts to colonize after displacing native Utah tribes with gridded Salt Lake City. The cool Mormons were doing Mormonism with music that was discordant, unnerving, and impossible. One spring night I got into a car with some of them headed to what became my first punk show, headlined by the iconic and ephemeral Minor Threat. Created from a place of rejection, trauma, and abnegation, punk felt uncanny, familiar, and became an integral part of my front-facing identity—I looked like I belonged to a new tribe, one that did not fit in, and one that most definitely challenged the expectations of a young Mormon woman. Finally embracing my weirdness, this iteration of musicking became a force that helped in sitting with my own troubled mother, other Mormons who felt askew in a culture of perfection. With my sister on drums, we started an ersatz band called Megawitch that debuted in Brigham Young University–approved student housing. My decades long participation in music, would for the rest of my life—as Joan references above—help me find little home bases wherever I lived, families I was not born into, but ones I found on my own.

And then I made my own. I was well into my thirties when my first child was born, after I'd left Utah and my church's American Zion for the still decidedly ragged lower east side of Manhattan. Why? Because I would be less likely to turn into a Mormon wife and mother there. Because it was a rock 'n' roll neighborhood, a place where the Ramones, Debbie Harry, GG Allin, and Patti Smith had created and roamed. My new spouse and I landed two blocks from Allen Ginsberg's pad, our most famous American beat poet who, like Patti Smith, had folded himself and his poetry into rock spaces for decades (until Patti left for the suburbs of Detroit for marriage and motherhood). The lower east side at the time was still cheap to occupy, unconventional, cramped, and "extreme." If I were to do "mother things," I wanted to do them there, in a dense, interesting place. One afternoon, I watched, hugely pregnant, with awe as Joey Ramone ambled his way towards me on East 9th Street in the East Village. My children played in Tompkins Square Park where Patti Smith first met Robert Mapplethorpe. Waiting for a bus on Avenue A, I made sure my kids knew we were standing adjacent to punk icon Richard Hell, from whom Malcolm McLaren swiped Johnny Rotten's look for the Sex Pistols. At home, we played the extreme music created in our chosen neighborhood. Science foregrounds how beneficial exposure to music and active participation in music is for a child's development and emotional health. But it was also important for me, and remains so. What forms this participation took while constricted by the demands of mothering is a crucial element in our study.

Joan and I are at least a generation and a half apart. We were raised on opposite sides of the continent and by very different mothers, but we felt an immediate kinship that went beyond our shared profession as librarians. In our mutual practice of musicking as mothers, in the ways in which our connections to extreme and hard music subcultures are crucial to how we are seen and how we see ourselves, we inhabit the same idiosyncratic mother gang. From our own research in related areas and anecdotal evidence, we knew there were others like us. What were their experiences? How did motherhood disrupt or enhance or trouble the various iterations of this identity?

Where could we find the written discourse of this unconventional and in our opinion, extraordinary and crucial experience?

We decided we would have to create the discourse ourselves, and make a space for this gathering of often marginalized voices. In her 2001 memoir *A Life's Work*, novelist Rachel Cusk asserts that the "experience of motherhood" loses everything in the translation to the "outside world" (2021, 3), and that mothering and the experiencing of motherhood should by necessity take place in private spaces, out of view. That there is something so essentially unnerving or just plain dull about it, Western culture seems to prefer not to see it at all. This is a notion that makes the act of caring for a child in public a radical act: for example, nursing a baby on the playground, changing a diaper in a precarious place—doing the necessary caregiving work in a context structurally resistant to it is theoretically fascinating, but in practice, is enraging and exhausting. Like every mother, "Mothers who Rock," or who at the very least want to publicly display their essential "rockness"—whether in their own public park or while pregnant while rocking on stage—necessarily experience dissonance, disjunctivism, and public pushback, as so many of the mothers in these studies have revealed in our interviews and within the pages of published memoirs. That the inherent marginalization of motherhood is something that's still being textualized in contemporary publications such as Cusk's is something this book hopes to address. This book challenges the idea that mothers should be hustled off stage and into the shadows, where the essential mother work can continue without any public resonance.

In 1971, Ellen Willis, the *New Yorker* magazine's first popular music critic, writes that "early rock" (and as it so happens, rock for decades after 1971) is sexist in ways almost too obvious to mention: from the fact that the majority of rock bands are male dominated in an industry almost entirely controlled by men, to song lyrics that "assumed traditional sex roles" and performers that "embodied them." But that in spite of all this, the music itself transcends the gender binary in that it's essentially about the revolt of "black against white," "working class against middle class," "youth against parental domination and sexual puritanism" (Willis 2011, 135). Willis goes on to articulate that despite the sexist iterations of the genre, the fact that female rockers and rock fans identify with rock's constructed maleness has been less about masochism and more about taking advantage of the moment "however possible": "For all its limitations," Willis writes, "rock was the best thing going."

Two decades later in 1992, rock 'n' roll mom Courtney Love may have been obliquely referencing Willis—and it would not have been a surprise—when she responded to Sub Pop co-founder Jonathan Poneman who interviewed Love and spouse Kurt Cobain for *Spin* magazine not long after the birth of their only child, Frances Bean. Poneman asks Love if pregnancy and new motherhood affected her "artistic perspective." Love's response is eviscerating and underscores a mother's need for access to extreme modes of expression: "What am I supposed to do, turn into fucking Mother Teresa all of a sudden? Am I supposed to write a country record because I had a baby? I've felt more sexual warfare, political, medical, and media terror in the last couple months than I've ever felt in my whole life" (Poneman 2017).

We'll posit that Love's response would have cheered the late rock critic Willis and given her hope regarding the future of women taking up space in conventionally male rock spaces, animated by what music critic Anwen Crawford refers to as rock's "phallic drive" (2015, 66). In Willis's 1974 essay "Women's Music" about the benign missteps of a scrappy women's music festival held at the University of Illinois, Willis's takeaway from the event is that what she most missed there was the presence of rock music. She writes that the programming exhibited a lack of popular music's aesthetic extremes. In Willis's words, the music of this women's music festival in 1974 seemed merely a reiteration of the music traditionally available to women—two forms only—folk and pop, and that neither of these, Willis argues, are vehicles for "active emotions—anger, aggression, lust, the joy of physical exertion—that feed all freedom movements" (2011, 143).

Willis's words, along with those of many other critics, feminists, musicians, and essayists that we have gathered here, combine to give us something of a baseline to analyze the thoughts and expressions of the spectacular rock and metal moms who are at the core of this book—an idiosyncratic subculture of women that includes those who musick in rock spaces when time and energy affords, to those whose front-facing rock identities may not be their livelihood but are essential to their sense of identity and well-being, to astounding international rock star mothers whose careers were built within misogynistic structures conventionally inhospitable to mothers and children.

Our book begins with an overview of women and heavy music and the ways in which women have historically engaged with musicking as mothers. We preface the limitations of this ongoing research and rock and metal's challenges with whiteness, situating our study in both an ethnographic and auto-ethnographic lens as musick mothers ourselves. Chapter 2 highlights and foregrounds powerful one-on-one original interviews as vignettes that narrate thematic patterns we saw arising from our musicking mothers. Chapter 3 extracts and analyzes the mothering narratives of famous rock moms, which are embedded in their respective published rock 'n' roll memoirs that we call the "rock mom memoir." Chapter 4 presents an auto-ethnographic context within which the concept of vigilante motherhood and how that is performed as mothers is investigated. Chapter 5 discusses daughters of rock moms and how music becomes a sight for bonding, and chapter 6 takes a look at the themes that arose, regarding how and what mothers write about when creating their own music. We conclude with the overall insights this study provided, while meditating on the historically marginalized moms we predict and hope the focus will be on for the future. This book is just the beginning. We look forward to what this book inspires and emboldens.

Chapter 1

Mother Framing

METHODOLOGIES

Framework

Women have always been active creators and participants in the music sphere, yet in the historical canon of most musical genres, the acknowledgment of their significant contributions is lacking (McClary 1991, 5). Interestingly, this doesn't seem to be the case in modern popular music, where women have been and still are very much in the limelight, yet their historical representation remains scarce within classical, rock, jazz, metal, and other musical genres. And in any genre, the struggle remains the same: In a 1979 edition of *Jazz Spotlite News*, hattie gossett with Carolyn Johnson writes that "many jazzwomen worked less frequently than they might have in order to spend more time with their families. After all, it's expected of a woman to do this, right? [. . .] and what about when you have your time of the month or when you're pregnant? Doesn't this all add up to a big deterrent?" (gossett 1995, 61). Perhaps in one of the most seminal texts about women and music, scholar Sheila Whiteley writes on the history of women musicians from the '70s citing " . . . both the lifestyle and the musical ethos of the period undermined the role of women, positioning them as either romanticized fantasy figures, subservient earth mothers, or easy lays." Such commentary points to the conventional norms to keep women musicians within very strong and controlled boxes.

If women *are* acknowledged in the press, it seems almost always negative in respect to body image and perception. This lack of representation has been explained by a number of scholars, most evident in the works of feminist ethnomusicologist Susan McClary. In her book, *Feminine Endings* (2002), McClary writes about the historical challenges women have faced in both musical participation and production, and the obstacles placed before them by society through stereotyped perceptions of their gender being weaker and unable to sustain creativity. Objectified and limited in their social musical activities, it seemed that many women have had to conform to societal expectations of their gender, (i.e., softer and melodic musical sensibilities befitting a feminine decorum) (McClary 2002, 9–12). In Western society, aspects of femininity and masculinity have been placed in binaries, whereby males are associated with characteristics of strength, aggression and power, and females are characterized in direct opposition: weakness, passivity, and impotence (Weinstein 2000, 67). In Extreme Metal Music (ENM) as well as other musical genres like Rock and Punk, these strong binaries work to reinforce cultural barriers and obstacles for women in a number of ways: sexualization, abuse/violence, and even the questioning of authenticity. For feminist musicologists like McClary, discussion of topics such as music, gender, and feminist critique have opened the doors for new investigations.

Most recently, women in interdisciplinary fields have taken up the mantle of writing about women and their participation within metal music offering a self-reflectivity that was lacking in previous studies conducted only by male scholars. To date, studies of metal in Canada (Kitteringham 2014), Texas (Vasan 2010), the United Kingdom (Riches 2011; Hill 2012; Shadrack 2014), and Tasmania (Phillipov 2012) have written explicitly on women and their involvement with metal and rock relative to their regions.

As an additional lack, there is a gap in the literature when one looks to research on parenting *and* music; in particular, mothering in the rock and metal subcultures has an intersectional piece to it all, as motherhood studies has typically been under researched in metal and rock subcultures. As mentioned in our introduction, the impetus of this study was our own experiences as mothers who participate in heavy music cultures, and the fact we noticed a dearth of literature on our own experience and those of women we knew and were beginning to interview. The few published resources that touched on the subject include Rita Gracio's article, "Daughters of Rock and Moms Who Rock: Rock Music as a Medium for Family Relationships in Portugal." In her paper, Gracio brings to light the ways in which musicking is transmitted from parent to child and how integral memories form to create a platform for family relationships: she writes, "rock music articulates more empowering versions of maternal subjectivities, and specific settings—such as car journeys—can constitute 'music asylums'" (Gracio 2016). This idea of experiences within musicking spaces (moments where music bonds happen between parent and child) came to light in participant interviews, as well as our own experiences of early music exposure.

Jilian Bracken's chapter, "A Discussion of Mothers' and Children's Roles in the Transmission of Music Listenership Values in Families," builds upon

Figure 1.1. Puma Perl in performance.
Source: Photo by Alice Espinosa-Cincotta

this concept of intergenerational music transmission, citing that discourse and engagement interactions hold importance on mother musicians and their relationships to their children through a strengthening of connection and bonding.

In working with our key terms "women," and "heavy music," and even "mothers," we must acknowledge that definitions can be limiting and are shifting, and that adhering to conventional definitions of these terms makes the discussion seem old-fashioned at best, at worst, part and parcel of patriarchal systems. And as we witnessed during Supreme Court justice Ketanji Brown Jackson's 2022 confirmation hearings, defining what a woman is, is not as simple as it seems. Jackson herself responded with "I'm not a biologist," which presupposes that it is biology that determines a woman. Defining what a mother is, is not as simple as it seems. Does any woman who has intermittently or otherwise "mothered" qualify? What about the rock guitar wielding aunt who had participated in the caregiving of a nephew? This was a question that was asked of us. Writing at a time when transmen can become mothers, when making assumptions about one's gender identity and pronouns feels ham-fisted, anti-nuanced, and retrograde, this study acknowledges the seismic shifts regarding challenges to the gender binary. Room must be made in our language and culture for the many iterations of gender—the myriad of articulations of "selves" in the world. Relatedly, this study also recognizes that there are self-identified, cis-gendered men occupying "mothering" spaces. With all this in mind, we acknowledge that our study of largely cis-gendered "women" who conceive, carry a child to term, and then endure the extreme experience of labor and delivery to then go forth into the maximum rock 'n' roll of a lifetime of mothering—well, it can't help but seem antiquated.

We acknowledge the limitations of a study formed by these conventional definitions, yet at the same time, much of the richness that transpired was a result of them. Further, we hope to do more. It might help to note that the limitations admitted here were part and parcel of the subjects we studied: the majority of mothers who responded to our survey, interviewed, and whose published narratives we analyzed largely represented the conventional binary. By extension, none of our subjects have spoken of their gender identity in ways that disrupt this conventional binary. This means that our study can be distilled down, in part, to the simple dynamic of "girls against boys." To speak like academics, we are interested in an old dynamic: a general, homogenous articulation of "femaleness" asserting itself within the monolithic male-dominated nature of heavy music genres. Of course, these are loaded females—rock women who mostly chose motherhood and who aren't necessarily sidelined by it. The participation of these women is sometimes a site of struggle, and always a site of complexity, and this creates the essential tension that defines one of this study's central questions: What are the ways in which mothers in rock and metal push back on the expectations and limitations of heavy music?

ROCK AND METAL'S WHITENESS

In addition to grappling with the problem of defining our terms, we acknowledge that a study on rock, metal, punk rock, and adjacent genres has an essential representation problem, and by that, we mean a racial representation problem. This was initially seen early on in the project as we gathered data from our online survey. Most of the mothers who completed this survey identified as white. Most of the mothers who sat for our face-to-face interviews were also overwhelmingly white, not to mention middle class, straight and cis-gendered. And we are, at this writing, still evaluating what this signifies. Perhaps this whiteness is related to racial biases in rock and metal music. Anyone who has attended a metal or rock festival, has a sense of the homogeneity of the genre. That rock music has a well-documented white supremacy problem is deeply disturbing and no surprise (Kelly 2020). In spite of the fact that rock and heavy metal music is a genre directly inspired by and built on the efforts and genius of Black blues musicians, the contributions of these musicians were co-opted from the beginning by a white-controlled music industry. A book about mothers, must include the formidable rock pioneer Big Mama Thornton, born in 1926, whose only hit "Hound Dog" was recorded in 1953 and written especially for her by iconic white and Jewish songwriting partners Leiber and Stoller. Those not in the know only know it as a smash for Elvis Presley, who re-recorded it as a "bright-eyed pop" track in 1956 (Gaar 2002, 1–4). What's deeply troubling is that the history of rock 'n' roll, which has augmented, enhanced, and even saved our lives as girls and young women and eventually mothers, has a deeply troubled and traumatic history. Thornton's story is only one of many in the history of disenfranchisement of Black artists in popular music. The debt that we owe Black women for the music that is at the core of this book is immense. Any story of women in rock starts with Black women.

WOMEN AND HEAVY MUSIC

Making heavy music for female artists may have been born out of some necessity to be taken seriously. Artists like Patti Smith and Chrissie Hynde emulated male rock rebels' toughness out of necessity: "it seem[ed] to be the only way to get what they wanted, to be free of the restrictions that trammelled women in pop" (Reynolds and Press 1995, 240).

Even a visually feminine Kate Bush embraces an iteration of rock aggression, music, conventionally coded as male that "puts you against the wall" [. . .] "I'd like my music to intrude," Bush asserts (Reynolds and Press 1995, 240–41). Generally speaking, women in rock historically act hard if they want to have authority and be accepted. Hard music "might be a place where every trace of the feminine has been expunged" (Reynolds and Press, 247). Music scholar Maureen Mahon writes that Black women artists, like Tina Turner, moved from conventional Black musical styles like rhythm and blues to covering popular hard rock tracks—essentially co-opting a white male stance—in order to break racial and sexual barriers (Mahon 2020, 254–55).

OUR STUDY'S METHODOLOGY

While Virginia Hanlon Grohl birthed a rock star in son Dave Grohl, and stories abound of mothers of musicians and the women who became infamous groupies during the heyday of rock, very few books explore the "lived" experience of women who are both musicians and mothers in their own right. While much of this chapter is populated with references to women who are musicians, this book explores the stories of women who are not only musicians, but also music academics, music fans, deejays and music writers. Their experiences with motherhood, and most particularly, music making and "musicking" culminate to form a very real, sometimes visceral and liminal experience for musical mothers in the rock and metal realms.

Using participant observation, semi-structured one-on-one interviews, and an online survey, we explore music-informed mother identity and the influence of cultural practice within rock and metal subcultures to provide an ethnographic lens. In exclusive interviews, presented as vignettes, we explore how musical mothering transgresses iterations of motherhood and how the participation of mothers challenges rock and metal masculinity. We aim to answer—why heavy music and mothers? How do tonal, political messages dovetail with gender and expectations of motherhood and allow for liminality? What is musical mothering and how does it influence cultural practice within rock and metal? Do musical dynamics play a role in family relationships and how can feminism navigate rock and metal masculinity while giving space for mothers and self-care?

This book's target audience are rock and metal academics, students in social science, cultural anthropology, gender, sexuality, and motherhood studies (both undergraduate and graduate). While we have synthesized our demographic data taken from the online survey (of which there were 194 respondents, representing a range of ages and geographical regions), we have opted to pull from our qualitative data that was gathered from our one-on-one interviews, which focused more on mothers (see interview table below) as musicians and fans and their links as participants in the rock, punk and metal subcultures from which they hailed. As researchers, we felt that a mixed methods approach to creating an ethnography would provide a richer lens and narrative of these womens' stories.

Table 1.1 outlines key demographic data for the qualitative interviews that were collected for our study over the course of about three years. The table in this chapter provides a brief overview—a bird's eye view, if you will—of the enormous amount of information in chapter 2 provided by a plethora of rock mom interviewees. The table provides a quick window into our qualitative data in terms of selected demographic data. While the online survey served to kickstart our research and widely publicize our study, we ultimately found our one-on-one interviews to be more valuable in providing a detailed and nuanced picture of these respective mothers' narratives and experiences, ranging in age, at the time of their respective interviews, from thirty-three

Table 1.1. Participants from one-on-one interviews

Participant	Age at interview	Marital Status	Musical Role	Number of children
Mallika	40	Married	Vocalist	2
Annie	35	Partnered	Music scholar, musician, and fan	1
Nicole	40	Married	Fan	1
Alexandra	33	Partnered	Fan	4
Mary Z.	56	Married	Bass player	2
Cynthia	65	Widowed	Bass player	2
Puma	Withheld	Widowed	Front person, spoken word, poet	2
Julie U	57	Single, Divorced	Lead singer, song writer	2
Emily	56	Married	Lead singer, guitar, lyricist	2
Sara W.	51	Married	Show host at MMH: The Home of Rock Radio	1 bio
Christy	53	Single, Divorced	Drummer	1
Dafna	62	Married	Vocals, guitar, composer, computer processing	2
Kari	58	Single	Record packaging designer, fan	1
Moan Elisa	40	Partnered	Guitar, rock band stylist	2
Darryl	54	Married	Fan, artist	2
Tanya	76	Partnered	Fan, mother of rock musician	1
Jessica H.	46	Married	Music journalist, author, director, producer	2
Dana	52	Married	Guitar, song writer	3
Nancy	59	Married	Makeup artist, fan, band member	1
Dana E.	64	Divorced	Fan, costume designer	1
Helixx	43	Single	Vocalist, lyricist	1

to seventy-six, with one mother withholding her age. While there is no column for race in table 1.1, roughly 80 percent of our participants identify as "white." Foregrounding this lop-sidedness connects to general whiteness of heavy music genres, at least in the United States in 2022.

Chapter 2

The Stories We Tell

QUALITATIVE INTERVIEWS (VIGNETTES)

Gathered here are transcriptions of our one-on-one interviews with rock 'n' roll mothers: heavy music lovers, on stage rock 'n' rollers, at least one heavy metal deejay, a rock critic, an artist or two or three, all heavy musicking women. Most of these interviews attempt to build a picture of what life and identity was like for these mothers before they became one, those identities disrupted by pregnancy, birth, child(ren). Maybe the impetus for this section, the blazing heart of this book, channels Celeste Bell, punk icon Poly Styrene's daughter. In the 2021 documentary Bell made about her mother, *Poly Styrene: I Am a Cliche*, Bell methodically assembles who her mother was before she became one: "Building a picture of who she'd been before me" (Bell and Sng). Likewise, our interviews here, at least in part, do some crucial work of recovery. Referencing a pre-mothering identity, many of the women whose interviews appear below admitted they were living full raucous lives, and were perfectly happy without children; furthermore, they weren't even sure they liked children. Some of them became mothers in spite of themselves, upending lives and order. Sheila Heti's 2018 novel, *Motherhood*, takes this a step further. In the novel, the narrator constantly challenges the line between Heti, herself, and a created persona, who wrestles, along the way, with whether "she" should become a mother or not. And that not having children is in itself a rebellious act. A woman without children threatens the social order:

> When I think of all the people who want to forbid abortions, it seems it can only mean one thing—not that they want this new person in the world, but that they want the woman to be doing the work of child-rearing more than they want her to be doing anything else. There is something threatening about a woman who is not occupied with children. There is something at-loose-ends feeling about

such a woman. What is she going to do instead? What sort of trouble will she make? (Heti 2018, 32)

However, referencing Heti's final line here, we often discovered in our interviews that these women made even more "trouble" in motherhood.

Previous to this book, listening to mothers was defined as incidental playground talk, which at times offered up unexpected and exquisite glimpses into pre-mothering lives, identities before maternal eclipse. These moments were often loci of pleasure and excitement: the mom who revealed she'd dated a bassist from a notable Los Angeles hair metal band and had hung out with an array of Sunset Strip rockers, for one. Mother connections of any kind are powerful, but mothers' stories can be astounding, especially in the playground. So the pivot from speaking to mothers as fellow sisters in shared spaces to occupying the "objective" position as "interviewers"—impassive ethnographers doing fieldwork—felt at once seamless and strange, and we touch on the problematic nature of this later on.

In many instances, the mothers we knew were the ones we'd found support and solidarity within our own motherhood journeys. Other times, we found ourselves sitting in front of mothers because of rock culture connections—and interviewing them was a breathless, fan-girl experience. In either context, being mother-to-mother was powerful. We sat down for interviews with mothers who had musicked in a variety of ways, for themselves, as part of an audience facing a stage, or performing for ardent fans—mothers who moved through the days holding the music close. Most of the women we interviewed would not be able to claim musicking as their main career. Still, their participation was meaningful, a necessity.

While the online survey that kicked off this study cast a wide geographical net, most of the one-on-one interviews were with mothers we'd met while mothering ourselves; we reached out to mothers found in New York City playgrounds, including the legendary Tompkins Square Park in Manhattan's East Village—quite possibly our country's most rock 'n' roll rock playground, an ersatz venue since the Grateful Dead played there in '60s, in a neighborhood that raucously and famously gave birth to punk rock in the '70s. This method of finding most—not all—of our interviewees meant that the sample was demographically limited in terms of race and class. Parents who are at leisure to linger in a rock 'n' roll playground either benefit from a supporting spouse, or have jobs that allow them the flexibility and privilege of raising their own children in one of the most expensive cities in the world. It has been important to us to continually remain conscious of the biases and often problematic structures that limited this study and kept it from possibly being as encompassing as it should have been.

What follows then are excerpts of interviews that lasted from thirty minutes to several hours. What we discovered is that all of these mothers formed musical identities in childhood/adolescence. And that a front-facing music identity was important to them whether they were conscious of it at the time or not.

The first two motherhood vignettes are Joan's and work to further contextualize these interviews. The remaining interviews are Julie's which are presented without other critical or theoretical voices.

VIGNETTE 1

When Self Is Selfless: Meaning Making and Motherhood

On identity:

> Absolutely certain. It is long gone. That's due in no small part to people dropping out of my life because I have a kid. But it's not just the metal scene, people from all walks of life—and activities of all kinds—aren't compatible with parenthood. (Annie, 2020 interview)

The mother-child relationship often relegates new mothers with a loss of self as cited above by one of our participants, Annie, a cis-white queer identifying woman who infers that mothering and musicking are antithetical to each other. At later stages of motherhood, many of our participants cited a return to self. It seemed that in order to navigate the balancing of a previous identity and motherhood, many women retreated into the mothering role alone. The self-awareness shown by Annie conveys how much she is aware of her own shaping of motherhood and its conflict with conventional norms of the child-centered caregiver.

> ... I had postpartum depression, on top of my husband losing his job the month after our son was born and so I was the sole income earner for a few months during my son's first year ... I don't think I knew where I was, let alone who I was, for the year or so after my son was born. But I realized that, for me, motherhood was a role, or a job, more than an identity. I had a lot of trouble with the concept of this one thing defining me ... (Nicole, 2019 interview)

> Honestly, I used to believe that motherhood was something incompatible with being a serious musician. I think this idea came from the fact that the most established and successful female musicians I knew of had decided against having children, or at least pushed it off to a later age, such as Doro Pesch and Angela Gossow. (Of course the implications of parenthood and pressures on men are

completely different, which points to societal inequalities, but that's another topic.) I didn't give much thought to reconsidering my opinion, until I got together with and married my current partner. Up until then I hadn't wanted to be a mother, I thought it was contrary to all my life goals, but our love for each other made me rethink everything . . . I still think it is very difficult to be a heavily touring musician with young children. However, I'm now aware that there are many other ways to be an accomplished musician that don't involve heavy amounts of touring, and that today in the digital age, post–Covid-19 times, it's much more possible to be a musician and have a successful career without touring six months or more a year. (Mallika, 2021 interview)

Certainly, this retreat or incompatibility that both Nicole and Mallika speak to benefit the patriarchal space of the male musicians who don't find themselves in the same parenting quandary as most female musicians. It isn't quite problematic for men who are fathers to opt out of touring as their women counterparts are usually left to parent the children. If you're able and financially stable to bring along an extra child-caring adult, then the *parenting while touring* challenge can be managed.

Our interviewees often spoke of the challenges of mothering on the road—the guilt and shame if they chose to leave their children in order to tour or the guilt to take them along for an unconventional childhood. Amy, vocalist and bassist of the metal band, Year of the Cobra, speaks on this same challenge:

So, touring, for me, is really difficult. I constantly feel guilty for leaving. For me, being a mother and a touring musician is like having a conflict of interests. I know that it's good for me mentally to have things that I do for myself. I know that music will be in my life forever; I will always play classical piano and I look forward to doing more of it when I have the time. I also believe it's good for my kids to see me doing things for myself. It's important for them to realize that I am an individual with needs and wants and interests and I hope that they are able to do that for themselves when they become adults and parents, if they choose to have kids. On the other hand, I feel so guilty leaving them for such long periods of time. They need me to be there for them, to raise them, and I want to be there for them. I don't want other people raising my kids. We have the option of taking them with us, perhaps homeschooling them and hiring a full time nanny to come tour with us, but then I feel like I'm taking away their childhood and dismissing their needs. (Amy, 2022 interview)

The duality of trying to occupy two spaces as mother and musician converge as a burden for these women. Patriarchy seems to demand that these women confirm to "good" mothering practices and be the nurturing and present mother that society deems acceptable. Fortunately, in Amy's case, she and her partner are able to support each other while on tour and parenting their two children, but this is not always the case, if at all. These similar experiences speak to the historical repression of mothers. The desire to be autonomous, creative, and the owner of their own futures sits antithetical within most musical subcultures.

VIGNETTE 2

Embodying the Visceral

Joan's Insights:

In her article "Scream Bloody Gore: The Abject Body and Posthuman Possibilities in Death Metal," Catherine Hoad writes that the musical genre of death metal is often regulated to having misanthropic and nihilistic lyrical themes, arguing that it's the same themes that enable a space of liminality for corporeality and the transgressive body. Building on this, much of our interviews with mothers in the metal music scene cited a similar experience in transgressive mothering. One very significant pattern arose with the idea of what could be more *extreme* than pregnancy and birthing? And the experience a mother's body undergoes to become both "other" and "abject body." But what do we mean by abject? Abject body defined by Julia Kristeva is the *human reaction (horror, vomit) of a threatened breakdown in meaning caused by the loss of the distinction between subject and object or between self and other* (Felluga 2011).

When I first started reading Kristeva, I was lost. But in a good way. I hadn't yet wrapped my head around her theory of abjection and alienation, but I knew that somewhere in her writings there was a connection to what some of our interviewees had described of their foray into motherhood. It started with gender, of being, of womaness, and then that of the changes of the body when a fetus developed. This foreignness, this difference/indifference, was something I myself remembered with my first pregnancy. I recall both the joy and fear I had watching my body grow another human being. A feeling of duality—happiness for creation and the sadness of losing a body that was my identity for thirty years. The growing alienation of something foreign was scary. I was considered high risk because of age and pre-existing diabetes. What if something went wrong? Would I be strong enough to keep this fetus to term? What if they were born with complications? Deformities? What if I was simply a "*bad*" mother? How do I reconcile not having maternal love or instinct for this new human? Would loving this new thing be natural? How could I even think of such a question?

> There looms, within abjection, one of those violent, dark revolts of being, directed against a threat that seems to emanate from the exorbitant outside or inside, ejected beyond scope of the possible, the tolerable, the thinkable. It lies there, quite close, but it cannot be assimilated. It beseeches, worries, and fascinates desire, which, nevertheless, does not let itself be seduced. (Jamieson 1990, 1)

Nothing reads more closely on Kristeva's quote above and the fears exhibited by so many women than the lyrics to the music of extreme metal (EM) bands. While EM has had a long history with engaging lyrics that are often nihilistic and morbid, it seems almost obvious that motherhood and the trials and tribulations that come with birthing connect with EM. Yet, there's quite a gap of women identifying these themes themselves in the musical compositions made by EM bands. The content and "gaze" here has been mostly male, white, and often misogynist. It's through our interviews, that a narrative began to emerge which speaks to a succinct group of women, both empowered and marginalized within metal and rock, a space in which we argue, like Kristeva, is both abject and object.

As Catherine Hoad explains, the ways in which the genre of Death Metal approaches the body, " . . . *as a site to be both celebrated and traumatized, liberated and conquered. Death metal's fascination with violence and horror,*" she argues, "*is at least partly born from a desire for transgression*" (Hoad 2012). Such insights fittingly dovetail with rock and metal mothers, who so often cited to us this need to fulfill their embedded natures of transgression: subjectivity that already places them living unconventional lives, being musicians in heavily male-dominated spaces and producing music that combats the status quo most often feminist in nature. Maternity is an experience that revolutionizes identity, consumes it, chews it, and spits it out. What remains for many women is a space that's often fraught with the imbalance of binaries:

> I find it interesting that during labor and childbirth (and beyond), we are at our most exposed, vulnerable, but at the same time our strongest, our fullest selves, and more aspects of our nature is revealed. I wish to go forward and show up to my life, and my art with this full spectrum of being. I think the most powerful and extreme art is something that rings true, (I think) it is produced when one connects to their innermost thoughts and emotions. (Mallika, 2022 interview)

How did our participants reconcile this vulnerability? Did they feel societal pressure that all things maternal should be natural; instinctual?

As Mallika says:

As it was something I hadn't envisioned for myself, it took a lot of learning and adjusting expectations, learning to be flexible, and finding balance. I didn't have good parental models growing up. My parents suffer with mental health issues and my childhood was very unstable and traumatic. I didn't want that life for myself and my children. (Mallika, 2022 interview)

Author Soraya Chemaly writes, "The physical transformation of a person's pregnant body, in a rapid and highly visible way, is material objectification. Pregnant women are stared at, commented on and touched; we belong to everyone" (Chemaly 2018, 98). I recall many times of my own pregnant body being policed, the lack of thought from comments and unsolicited advice given from strangers. This absence of agency for pregnant women leaves many alienated and reduced to just a vessel. Many of our participants claim this lack of ownership and agency. They were unconventional from the get-go, often citing how as musicians, their identities as women in overwhelmingly white and male spaces enforced a need to assert themselves. "I'm already different. You really don't hear about the laurels of female drummers" (Nicole, 2021 interview).

Figure 2.1. Julie Unruly fronting High & Tight.
Source: Photo by Anne Husick

Chapter 2

VIGNETTE 3

Cynthia, founding member of the 'B' Girls, bass player—the Renegades and New York Junk:

I've been into music probably since I saw the Rolling Stones on the *Ed Sullivan Show* in the '60s. I had a very physical and emotional response to that performance. I played piano starting at age seven, and was at conservatory at grade six, and took ballet for a long time as well. I remember the feeling of physically responding to music. At the age of twenty-one in 1977, I formed the 'B' Girls, an all girl four-piece rock band, in Toronto. I've seen so many documentaries on women who have made it on a much larger scale than the 'B' Girls did. We never compromised on anything because we were never a band that was put together by a guy. A lot of all girl bands gave up a lot of their creative autonomy. I think it's part of why we weren't successful in that way.

In New York in 1985, when I was about to give birth to my daughter Amanda, I told the doctor I needed to leave for five hours to play a gig with the band I was in, the Renegades. So I gave birth and went and played the gig when my baby was still in Beth Israel hospital. We were opening for Johnny Thunders at Irving Plaza. I think I must have been on the adrenaline rush of giving birth. What was going through my mind was what people would say about being a girl in a band—I didn't want people to say that you couldn't have a girl in the band because, what if she got pregnant? So giving birth was not going to stop me either. I had my husband, Billy, bring my gig clothes to the hospital. I had been rehearsing the whole time I was pregnant. I feel like in the womb that Amanda was listening to the Renegade's songs. She had access to the sounds of the bass guitar at my womb. And she did play bass in high school for a short time.

I was playing music consistently until then, and played in other bands with my husband Billy Rogers who was a drummer, who had played with Johnny Thunders and the Ramones. We moved to Canada when my daughter was nine months old. I took a break after I had my son—he was born in 1987. I kept playing through to the early '90s. Then the focus of my life changed. Becoming a mother comes with a lot of responsibilities and priorities. You can do it all, but not all at once. Music became something that was a secondary thing rather than a primary thing. Billy went right back to music and I became a single parent so I didn't have that option. I took a fifteen-year break from music, actually an almost seventeen-year break. It got to the point that when the kids were in their early or middle or late teens, I wasn't playing at all. I had high pressure jobs working for the city of Toronto on homelessness issues. My focus was on being a really good parent and making the world better.

In about 2002 or so, I started taking yoga with Xena, who had been a second singer in The 'B' Girls. I took yoga teacher training from her for the year. I wasn't playing music or doing art at all. I was being totally responsible and doing what was best for everyone else except myself. On a yoga trip to Peru with Xena, I had this awareness during some yoga sessions. I felt like I could actually see that person sitting in the corner. It was that young girl who dreamed of doing whatever she wanted to do, which was music and art and writing. Just sitting there in the corner, crying. I spoke about it and wrote it down and wanted to go get that sad girl crying in the corner. My whole energy around my creative self centered in New York City somehow. It was where it all coalesced. Where I felt like my true self. Where everything had happened with The 'B' Girls and CBGB in the '70s. Where the energy sparked. I started coming back down to New York in 2006 and playing with [Renegades' guitarist] Joe Sztabnik in his basement. I was going back and forth: Living in Toronto and working this responsible job, which allowed me to fly back to New York to do music.

My identity as a mother has receded more now that my kids are older, in their thirties. I don't have to worry about their priorities. I just have this internal thing. Now that I'm in my sixties and a grandparent. It's only been the last few years that I'm starting to feel more of a desire to spend time with family, as part of the balance of my priorities. Feeling a reconnection with that part of me. But I have been thinking a lot about societal "reality constraints" on what a woman can and can't do. Women have to morph into something else so many times. When I was in The 'B' Girls, we were known in the CBGB's scene, but like many of the bands that played there, we weren't part of the mainstream. And the band members felt they had to make a choice. Many of them did not engage in long term love relationships or become mothers. Because they felt that the two things were incongruous. Men can do it all that at once. Even just the physical thing of being pregnant for nine months disadvantages women.

The 'B' Girls—the way we existed was feminist. We wrote our own songs. We learned how to play our own instruments. We booked our own gigs. We never got gigs because we were girls. We got them because of our ability. I never felt marginalized within myself. But I do believe the world has constraints around you.

VIGNETTE 4

Julie Unruly (music identity name), lead vocalist, songwriter—High & Tight:

I've always suffered from extremely low self-esteem. I'm the child of a Holocaust survivor, and there was a lot of trauma in my childhood. Even though I don't have stage fright and consider myself an extrovert, I didn't like the way I looked, struggled with my appearance. It was always important to have a musical identity. I grew up playing the cello, and have always identified as a musician. I always went to shows. Listened to music. Followed it. Music has always been an important part of my life, and was always on in our home growing up. If I'd been a different person, more confident in who I was, I would have gone off on my own and been a professional musician, instead of in my spare time, as a hobby. I don't know why it didn't occur to me to be a rock star. I've always been a poet and a writer. I was an English major, and became an attorney. I didn't

Figure 2.2. Cynthia Ross on stage at Irving Plaza, New York City.
Source: Photo by Johan Vipper

realize I could write songs. I could have been Carole King of the punk scene. I'm pissed about the fact I didn't have the balls to do that. I have a friend I've known since I'm in college. I say to her, "Why didn't I write songs when I was nineteen?" She said, "You had to live your life."

I had my twins when I was forty. And after I had the kids, I got divorced, and spent a long time raising them single. When I started dating again, I dated a musician. He was like, "You play the cello? Well, you could play the bass.

I'm going to bring over a bass guitar." He'd been in bands since high school. It was his lifestyle. He taught me a couple of songs: "Dead Boys" was probably the first song I learned. It was so easy to pick up, because my ear is trained. And I started jamming with my boyfriend. He was the pivotal person. We made a band, Little Bombs. He had other bands and was all hooked in, and we started getting gigs. Playing out. Having a band lifestyle. When we split up, the band broke up. I was like, "Holy shit, I don't have a band. I have to have a band." It became my hobby, but it was more about my mental health. Having a band. Having the discipline. Having the camaraderie. Having the performance. Getting out there in front of people.

Music is my escape. Self care. I have rehearsal at a set time. I can't just blow it off. They always say mothers should take care of themselves. You can easily say, "I'm not going to take a bath." But when you're in a band, you can't let your bandmates down. There were times I felt I couldn't go to rehearsal because my daughter wasn't doing well. Also, I thought at the time I started doing it, my kids were around nine, and I thought it was a good example to set for them: "Mommy is here for you, but mommy needs to do things that make her happy so she can be a better mom. Not that you're not the center of the universe."

Recently, my son asked me, "How was rehearsal? Did you have fun?" It's a comfort for them to know I have a thing that makes me happy. So I feel it's important to show them that it's never too late to do something. Your life is an adventure, no matter what. My involvement in music is a very positive. I've dealt with so many dark things, it's been a positive light. Music has always been that. Always there for you. That's how that started. My twins saw the change and saw how happy it made me. It was weird and cool and a really good example to them that you should always have their own thing.

When I heard punk rock as a teen, it resonated with me. It was irreverent and loud. I was born in 1965. We were told we could do whatever the fuck we want. But that was a lie. You had to do it in a traditionally feminine "Ally McBeal"—lady attorney—way. But I'm loud, I'm clumsy, I'm messy. I have opinions. I have emotions. Our society doesn't tolerate that in women. Punk rock was the acceptable way to be that way. As a woman who has always been told I'm "too much," I fell in love with punk rock. I love the spontaneity and improvisation and joy of it.

It has been life changing for me to have High & Tight. I write about shitty cab drivers mansplaining my own directions. Running out of vodka and having to deal with kids. Being a MILF. That I'm too much. Being a mom in a nuclear holocaust. Thinking about my son having diabetes. Wanting a better boyfriend. All the things that as a woman you deal with. My whole point is to look at what the fuck I'm doing. Are you kidding me? You'd better be laughing and having a good time. I write about how people need to open their mouths. Expanding it out to not just women, but just everybody. No time to be polite anymore. The kids are still very proud of it. They've seen High & Tight at least twice. They were like holy shit. I know that they know how important it is to me.

Figure 2.3. Emily Duff, pregnant.
Source: Photo by Pat Kepic

VIGNETTE 5

Emily, guitar, vocals, songwriter—The Emily Duff Band:

> I never planned on being a mother. I hate kids. I don't like kids. I grew up in a very dysfunctional family. My joke is that I was raised by a pack of cigarettes. Not even a pack of wolves. My mother's father died of alcoholism. He literally froze on the street on a winter night from drink.

I wanted to be a songwriter from the time I was seven when I wrote my first song about baseball cards. I started playing mandolin at four, guitar at the age of six. My mother taught me four chords. I was completely obsessed with Johnny Cash, Janis Joplin, Laura Nyro, and Neil Diamond. The Brill Building meant everything to me. I was born in 1966, and got to experience a golden age of music.

My perspective completely shifted when I became a mother. Before I was writing songs that now I look back and go, "That's whiney, navel gazing, narcissistic shit." And now I'm writing stuff that connects me with more people, because my topics are now a bit more universal. As a mother, I feel like I have a responsibility now as a writer to convey a message of a little bit more love and kindness, because I'm trying to seed a different vibe in the world that my children will live in long after I'm dead. I'm trying to get people vibrating on a different frequency of a little less selfishness.

When I was pregnant with Sylvia I played up until about four weeks before I delivered and I got up on stage and you couldn't tell I was pregnant facing head on or from behind. But from the side I looked like Warren Haynes from the Allman Brothers—That's what some guy said to me at a bar. And I literally had someone say to me, "You shouldn't get up on stage pregnant because there is nothing sexy about that. That is not rock and roll." Being on stage and being in that role of rocker as a life giving, gestating maternal, there ain't nothing sexy about you, get off the stage, I can't objectify you. You make me feel uncomfortable. Men would get angry with me when they would see I was pregnant and playing in a club and felt I had no business being there. It made them say things to me like, "Oh, yeah, you're going to be a great mother."

I never saw being a rocker and being a mother as something viable, which is interesting because I was also a chef. And you really can't do chef/mother at the same time either. Because you need freedom and you need your body and those are the two things you really give up when you become a mom. And then eventually, if you're lucky, you get your freedom back in a certain way, but your brain never stops being a mother. You're wired differently for the rest of your life.

And that affects the music positively if you allow it to. You can fight it. You can start writing kids music and then you're an idiot. People ask me all the time, "Now that you're a mom, are you going to do music for kids?" And I was like, "What the fuck is that?" That's like a child's menu. There's no kid food. There should be no kid music. My daughter wound up learning the days of the week from the Clash song "Police on My Back." I'm never going to do kids music and I'm never going to teach children. I'm never going to give guitar lessons.

I watched the *Sonny and Cher* show as a kid and either Sonny or Cher would bring Chasity out at the end and hold her, and I thought, "YES! I wanna be a mum like that."

Fuck yes, there's still a lot of sexism in the music industry. I mean I walk down the street and people still say to me, "Oh, are you going to your lesson?" "No. I'm a recording artist. I get reviews in big magazines." I walk into a club and even my band does this to me. I'll be setting up a PA. The guys in my band even say, "Oh, no, it goes there. You put the plug in there and I'm like, no you don't!" I know how to do this. I've worked in recording studios. I always get why I get this. As long as I have boobs, I'm only going to be second guessed. And if you show a little bit too much, then the focus is immediately taken off your music. I'm not going to get on stage in a potato sack because I like wearing beautiful clothing—leather pants. There's something about leather that automatically makes you feel very sexy, so you want to get on stage and feel confident—and part of that is feeling sexy, but sometimes you feel a little bit self-conscious and guilty about putting yourself out there. So you can't feel responsible for changing someone's mind about how people have been thinking for thousands of years. But I have recalled times where I have gone onstage and thought they might just be looking at my boobs. I might have done myself a disservice. They might not take me seriously right now.

In my opinion, there is nothing more rock 'n' roll than being on stage with another human being inside of you. First of all, I never felt better in my life than I did when I was pregnant. No morning sickness. Nothing. If I could be pregnant all the time in that type of healthy, energetic . . . I felt like Lindsay fucking Wagner as the Bionic Woman. I had energy. I felt great. I had horrible labors and then C-sections. My body doesn't want to be in labor or deliver, but pregnancy, I was born for it. Coming into motherhood, your shift is enormous. My style changed. My music changed. Pre-motherhood, I had been a lot heavier, musically. I was a rocker. And then all of the sudden, there was a gravitation from electric guitars and boxes and effects and pedals to an acoustic guitar, completely stripped down, bare and vulnerable, and that is not a coincidence. There are layers that just get peeled off of you once you have had a baby. It's elemental. This is you stripped down to your bare essence as mother. That's what I became as a musician as well.

VIGNETTE 6

Puma Perl (music identity name), vocalist, lyricist—Puma Perl and Friends:

On a logistical level, I was most affected by motherhood when I had to leave the Lower East Side for Brooklyn for a number of years to accommodate the kids. When I was still in the Lower East Side it was easier to get out. At the same time, there were certain areas of my life that would not be considered rock 'n' roll, like poetry and Latin music, places I was able to bring my kids. Even in Brooklyn, I took them to outdoor shows and some concerts, but they were hard to afford. I also needed to further my education and worked a demanding full-time job, so all of those factors kept me from being an active participant in the rock 'n' roll scene. Even Patti Smith took a long sabbatical to raise kids. And even among women we know locally, many of them left the scene for various lengths of time to raise, and often, find a way to support kids, and returned when the situation became more viable. We see less of that among men.

Men almost never change their lives to care for children. They are the ones on the road when there is a couple with children, for the most part. My personal experience as a performer is not unlike my world experience. The guys who work with me in Puma Perl and Friends usually follow Joff Wilson's lead and he's always been clear that they are painting my words with music. In a broader sense, of course, men are allowed to get old and still be attractive and are not judged on their looks the way women are. But again, this is the world we live in. Maybe it's getting a little better. I think people are not saying "female drummer" as often as they used to, as women are taken more seriously as musicians and are occupying the stage, leading bands, and writing songs. Well, they always wrote songs but were often overlooked by the bands they played with—like the Revolution with Wendy and Lisa. Maybe we need a Guerrilla Girls type group to focus on the rock world the way they do with the art world and provide hard statistical facts.

But it does seem that there are probably a greater percentage of female rockers who reached success who remained childless, than in the general population.

VIGNETTE 7

Sara Whizbanger (music identity name), professor, radio programmer, and show host—The Whizbanger Show on MMH:

I was born into rock 'n' roll. My dad is David Bennett Cohen. He played keyboards for Country Joe and the Fish. He was at Monterey Pop. He still plays music. I needed to find my own way. My dad was into Dr. John, so I decided I was not into Dr. John. My dad was into outlaw country, which meant I hated it. Now it's like my go-to. I play that shit on my show. When your parents are kind of cool, and your mom is into rock 'n' roll, and your older siblings are into punk rock, I had nowhere cool of my own to go. I was raised on rock 'n' roll, punk rock, blues, outlaw country. I had this wide field in which to frolic. When I was eight, nine, and ten, I was discovering music for myself. I was into Pat Benatar, Blondie, AC/DC, Rush, Devo, the Clash, and then I found Sabbath.

I grew up having a voice. I was never treated less than for being a girl, or different because I was a girl. I kept up with my brothers. That still holds true. When I came out as not being straight, my family was like whatever. It wasn't an issue. Berkeley is an interesting place to grow up. Growing up around people of color, around queer people was always part of my landscape. My brothers used to take me to shows in the Bay Area where we lived. My first show was DOA and Siouxsie in 1980. I was ten years old and I wanted to leave. I remember feeling like everyone was really dirty and gross. I never had a life without music. Music has been part of my landscape since I was in utero. My dad was friends with Janis Joplin. She held me when I was a baby. My dad said she was absolutely in love with me. She was so happy my mom had a girl and she came over when I was a few months old shortly before she died and held me at arm's length with a cigarette hanging out of her mouth.

    I was twenty-four when I became a mother. Motherhood was not something I wanted to happen in my life. I love kids, I relate to them. I enjoy babies. I didn't want one. My upbringing was tumultuous and unsafe. My father was a cocaine dealer. My mom has borderline and narcissistic personality disorder, like intense. I grew up with a lot of emotional abuse, and my dad put me in a lot of unsafe situations, at the same time, being very proud of me, always bestowing love on me and providing for me, but also putting me in harm's way every single day of my life, up until I was a teenager. I ran away a lot. I was in and out of the San Francisco court system. I was a ward of the court. I was not safe until I was well into my twenties and living on my own. I still have a feeling of general unease in my life. I have built-in fear that exists in my core from my youth. So I didn't want kids. I knew I had zero examples. I knew if I had a kid, I would be totally on my own. I wouldn't have a mother or a father to help me, although that has changed over time. My dad has done a lot of internal work. The chances of meeting some dude who actually had his shit together in our scene was next to nil. It wasn't that I didn't want kids, I just didn't think it would ever happen for me, and I didn't think it would be a good idea.

    I remember the day I got pregnant. I had sex with my boyfriend, condom off. And I looked up at him, and said, "I'm pregnant." I just knew. That happened more than one time on the pill. A few weeks later, I did a pregnancy test in the bathroom at my college, I did a pee test and that was it. I just sat there and cried and cried, and I was so incredibly happy and excited. I let that feeling take over. I loved being pregnant. I wasn't freaked out about it at all. The birth was "textbook" 12.5 hours of labor. I had a midwife and she was great. My doula was there. The doctor who was there was really cool and let everyone do everything until Devon came.

    I have the same musical identity I've had since I was twelve when I decided I was a rocker. That was how I identified. My world was heavy metal. That identity didn't recede at all. I never felt like because I was a mom I needed to behave a certain way. I took Devon to their first show at the Pignic put on by Wavy Gravy every year. Devon's first show was Spearhead and I had them on my shoulders in the pit and we were dancing around. I've never had a life without music. Music has been part of my landscape since I was in utero. My parents were at Woodstock, but didn't play. What do you say when you know Janis Joplin was in love with you when you were a baby and held you when you were a baby? Music just is.

    Devon didn't grow up on Disney. No Raffi. I didn't let them have any gun toys in the house. We had Cheech Marin's *School Bus Driver* cassette. *Free to Be You and Me*. I gave them stuff that I had as a kid. When they were six, they really loved the Bad Brains and listened to them all the time. I remember finally being like, "No more Bad Brains." I can't believe I'm actually putting a moratorium on one of the greatest bands of all time. They were really into KISS. Devon sought out their own musical identity when they were a teenager, and now they're super into goth and dark wave stuff, and DSBM, which they tell me staves off depression.

As I was carving out an identity as a mother, I was also carving out an identity as an adult. I was a kid, twenty-three when I got pregnant. It's only becoming clear to me now that I have all this PTSD because I'm only now post-traumatic. Now that I'm in this healthy place in my life I can reflect on that. I was in trauma at the time of Devon's birth and much of their life.

My parents never supported me in any passions. They were also so completely checked out and wrapped up in their own identity and their own lives that I was an afterthought. When I was growing up and being a mom at the same time, I often say, I parented "by Braille." Every choice I made as a parent, I thought about what I would have done and did the opposite. I wanted Devon to have total freedom to choose and I may have done that too much. I tried to involve them in everything. I showed up for everything they did, every performance, every game, and I encouraged them but I didn't try to push them in any direction. Is that a regret? I don't know. I was a total helicopter mom because I was always afraid someone was going to take them away from me for all their life. That drove my presence in their life pretty intensely. I didn't know how to encourage them to pursue a particular thing without feeling like I was being pushy. That's a hallmark of insecurity and being a young adult, who is not old enough to have a kid yet. But the thing that went through my head was, this is your one shot to have a kid. I may not have ever done it again.

It's interesting being who I am now, and the age I am now, with a child who is twenty-seven years old. My relationship with them now is very good, very honest. We can have open conversations about their childhood. I know the one thing I did right was create someone who was going to be honest with me. With these kids now and embracing gender fluidity, it's the best thing that could happen in this world. They don't give a shit, it doesn't matter.

Heavy metal and motherhood, for me, I don't know. I like a lot of different music. I even like pop music. I feel like music has really shaped me. If I want to do an arc of analysis of what I listened to during my life, I could make direct connections to how a particular album influenced me at the moment. I remember discovering the Scorpions back catalog from before I knew they existed, and Black Sabbath, Priest, and Iron Maiden. That would be a really interesting thing to do, an autobiography based on albums and songs. When I discovered heavy metal was about the time my life really went sideways in terms of my safety, my drug use, and running away, dropping acid, cutting class. I was going to shows and that's where I was safe. Showing up at Ruthie's Inn at twelve, thirteen, fourteen years old was the safest place for me, and part of that was because of my brothers who were a decade older than me. All these people were looking out for me. Rick from Exodus was on my show and says he remembers me in those places as a kid. Those were the people who protected me. Back to feminism and being a girl in the scene, my experience is unique, because of my brothers. When Riot Grrrls came around and started talking about violence against women, I was like "What the fuck are you talking about?" I teach Kathleen Hanna's *The Punk Singer* for my course on Storytelling and Film. We discuss how problematic this scene was and continues to be. That's not to discount the fact that some of these women experienced horrible homophobia from their parents, or domestic violence or incest. They came into our scene and claimed it as their own, and pretended none of us young women who had already been there mattered. That's the part that bothers a lot of people. We were already fucking here. We've been doing this for fifteen years already. Do you not know who Lydia Lunch is? And Becky Bondage? I'm a sociologist, so I live and breathe context for a living. I can't think of a Riot Grrrl scene without thinking about my experience and the experience of the people around me. There was already not a whole lot of people of color in a scene that was in a city populated with many people of color. Not only did they silence older punk veteran working class white women who had been there for fifteen years, but they made invisible our women of color compatriots, and made their personal narcissistic issues—again, not to dismiss their experience—the main event. And we didn't exist. None of us were invited into that conversation. They made the blunder that our parents' generation made, which was to leave men out of the conversation about feminism in the '70s. Feminism invites them to understand who they are as husbands, who they are as fathers, what their contributions can be. Here we are, the secondary children of the revolution, and they got it wrong and we have an opportunity now to be in more inclusive dialogue around that. You can't take men out of the equation if you're going to talk about feminism. It punished us as working class kids. Riot Grrrl, however, did carve a space for more women to be involved in punk and metal, which I think is great.

My friend Stephanie used to have an all black metal show after my show on MMH. Now she does a show with me called "Sound of the Whizbanger Underground," and we do specials every few months. The last one we did was the "Top 40 Disco Hits of Black Metal." We played the artist Midnight. They have very sexually explicit lyrics, not in a way that's abusive to women, but they're just super dirty and raunchy sex, and we're like, "You know what? Women like raunchy sex and that's cool." I feel like those really challenging questions about women being into porn, and rough sex, and being dominated—the limiting idea that only way women relate to that is because they have daddy issues or are the product of a toxic environment is fucking bullshit, because it takes away our sexual agency.

I went to Mills College and took this class called feminism and social ethics. I had been a stripper and a dominatrix in New York City in the early '90s. Stripping was fun. A lot of my friends showed up and gave me good tips. But at Mills I reflected on this experience. We were reading Andrea Dworkin, and I was going to take issue with this. I told my professor about my sex work, and the professor had already decided about me. It was terrible. She said, "I'm so sorry for you." And I'm like, for what, it was awesome! She would not listen to me. Maybe that's the next step in your research, asking what feminism looks like in heavy metal? How do we identify not just feminism, but also sexuality in the context of heavy metal?

In my work with deejays, you navigate this world of rock 'n' roll without anyone seeing what you look like. So it has to come in through the mic, your voice, and what you say. How do you build that personality when people can't see you? One of the women I talked to told me she heard her voice launched a million boners. Men don't hypersexualize themselves in a rock deejay context the way they do onstage. Where you have the tongue hanging out and the cock grabbing. That explicit pandering to masculinity. Part of being a deejay is that you are relating to people. I'm the deejay you feel like you're in a conversation with. People tell me when they listen, it's like they're hanging out with me. And that's what I want. Other people cultivate personalities. That gets into identity construction and cultivating an audience. For cultivating an audience in heavy metal, you're probably going to mostly have dudes. I do try with my *Hot Flash Friday* show to bring women's voices into the radio. Not just female fronted, but women in heavy music. That in and of itself is feminist. I've been a deejay for two and a half years. I first did it for a station that's now defunct called Metal Nation Radio. Friends in Calgary who were deejays brought me in. And I could do it at home. The next show I did was a Queercore show, very Judas Priest forward. I played "Ram it Down," like the gayest Judas Priest songs.

Music for self-care? Windhand, I will listen to them for many, many several hours. Judas Priest. Black Sabbath. Portishead. Red Garland. Tragedy. Sepultura—any Sepultura, I'm not a purist. I like all of it. But it really depends, sometimes I like to be nostalgic with music and sometimes I need Dorthia Cottrell [Windhand vocalist] to save me from myself.

VIGNETTE 8

Christy, drummer—Slowness, Gold:

My first recollection of feeling passionate about music was when I was in Virginia in sixth grade and my sister had recordings by the B-52s, the Police, and the Go-Go's. Billy Joel. My parents liked Herb Alpert. My mother liked Parliament, oddly enough. I became excited about music probably around sixth grade. In the '80s, I discovered post punk and new wave. I play guitar and sing. I've been a lead singer and a drummer in a band. But drumming is the thing people ask me to do with them.

When my dad was a career marine and I spent my junior year in high school in Newport, Rhode Island, and I happened to take classes with members of Throwing Muses—which used to be the Muses—and Tanya [Donelly] and Kirstin [Hersh] made me mixtapes of music I'd never heard before, and seeing their band was when I knew I wanted to be in a band. They let me play drums once at a rehearsal. And that's when I started playing drums. I was about seventeen years old. My very first band was a band called Balzac Frowning in

1989. Indie rock. Distorted guitars. Female vocals and that eventually morphed into Barbie Complex, which was a band that played at New York City venues Brownies, the Continental.

I didn't always want to be a mom. When I was a teenager and young adult, I didn't really envision having children. I didn't think I would have children. It wasn't something I was coveting. While I was with Charles, that sparked my interest in being a parent. I was around his nieces and nephews. I liked being around children and knew we would liked parenting together.

Ironically, when I was pregnant, I was playing in three bands, and playing all the time. I took almost no break after giving birth. I did go through a major identity issue after giving birth. I was pretty much a stay-at-home mom. Maybe a month or two I wasn't really playing but one of the bands I played with, the cellist got pregnant and had a baby two weeks before I did, so we would go to Rebecca's place and rehearse with our babies.

Remaining in bands turned everything around. I had all these identity issues as a new mother—all of the sudden, I'm a milk machine. I loved being a parent, but I was playing so much beforehand that I was afraid it was all going to dissolve during motherhood. Unless you're making money and have a touring nanny, it's really hard to keep doing music.

VIGNETTE 9

Dafna, vocalist, guitar, music processing, composer:

I've been a working musician since I was in my twenties, but did not have a kid until I was almost forty. My mother was always like you need to have a kid. It's important. Your life will be better and different and you need to know what it means. My mother was a radical feminist so it's not like she's coming from a sexist place. She was pushing for me to do it on my own. I said, "If I were a lawyer and I could afford full time care, maybe." Hans and I got pregnant after about ten days of knowing each other. So I had an abortion. Right now I think it's important to be open about it. Then after we eventually got married, we decided to have a kid. I turned forty a couple of weeks after Katya was born, and I was like, "Oh, shit. My life is not my own anymore. I can't decide when I'm going to do things. I'm not going to get any sleep. I don't know if I can be an artist. How am I going to do this?"

During the pregnancy, I kept performing. There was a gig I did at Roulette, where I remember someone saying, "Are you going to need an ambulance outside?" I remember being at Phill Niblock's Experimental Intermedia loft when I was five months pregnant and these were big loud events. The volume is the same as at rocker events. He has four big speakers in quad and I was sitting next to one of them and this guy I know from Paris was playing and all of the sudden, I feel Katya kicking me in utero, and I thought, "This is a distress call. And I was thinking about those PSAs from the '70s, "This is your brain on rock music," and they show these rats running around until they die, and so I went into the kitchen and she stopped kicking. And then I went back out, and clearly she was like someone with a broom handle, "Could you keep it down?" That would have happened if I'd been playing rock, too. At least 110 decibels. I was doing a lot while I was pregnant. We recorded that record with Kitty Brazelton when I was five months pregnant.

Being a mother has affected my career in every way. If we were in Europe this would be a totally different conversation. Musicians don't get free childcare here. Many of the musician women I knew who were moms had one child, not two. I almost knew nobody who had two kids like me. When I was having a baby I only knew Kitty [Brazelton]. She had one. The other women I knew who had children were composers, which is a different thing entirely. Composing as a mom doesn't involve other people. I did not have hours and hours like a male composer with no kids or obligations. So you have three hours and the kid's asleep, and you can compose. You can't do that if you're trying to book a rehearsal, with other people, all these moving parts. It's one of the reasons I ended up just doing duos. Otherwise, it was just too complicated. I once asked for a late soundcheck time in 2001 at the Kitchen after Katya was born and I got pushback until that person had her own kids. I was paying a babysitter. The fact that I would have to spend $100 if I wanted to go out and play with my partner. Otherwise, one of us had to be home. You can't do a lot of gigs unless you're independently wealthy. What I'm trying to say is that working on something just for yourself is not as hard, but when it involves a lot of moving parts and soundcheck. . . . Those who don't have kids may not understand why you're demanding the latest soundcheck before the show or the earliest one so you can go home and nurse the baby.

Around the time I was going to have Katya, Marina Rosenfeld was doing this thing called Sheer Frost Orchestra with all women on electric guitars, playing with bottles of Sheer Frost nail polish. She asked if I could do it and I said, "I'm supposed to be having a baby that week." She asked, "Do you know any other women?" And I said, "Yeah, except Mari Kimura is having a baby that week, too." I did come to the show with Katya; she was like two weeks old. I got into Djerassi, this great artist's residency in California, but it started in March and I was due April 15th. And I said, "I can't." And they said, "We've never had anyone turn it down for that reason. How about you come six months later?" And I said, "Great, I can bring the baby!" And they said, "No." Maybe a guy can come six months after they've become a father, but why would I have a baby and then leave it in New York so someone else can feed it with a bottle and I go sit in a room having deep thoughts?

Hans went on tour. I didn't go on tour. I didn't want to go on tour for years. Certainly not while my kids were nursing. I wouldn't miss a birthday. I can give you a big list of gigs and opportunities I've turned down, and I don't regret anything. My mother got her doctorate, but that means she was in the library; she wasn't available to us. There were a lot of things I wish she had been there for us more, but I don't blame her because it was awesome what she did. I mentioned that story about the residency to another artist, and I mentioned it was family unfriendly, and she said, "We all make our choices," And I was like, "Yeah, okay, but it is possible that the residency could do more for families," and now ten years later, fifteen years later, they are more open to that. Because mothers are speaking up.

If you're a parent, your time is limited. You can't be an artist and pay a sitter $15 or $20 an hour just to stand around waiting for a soundcheck. When I did a show in Holland they had a babysitter, but I could hear Katya crying from the stage. And I felt like, "Oh my God, why am I doing this?" I could hear her crying! I had to block it out and just play. And I can't say, "Hey, I'm sorry I'm going to leave the stage now because that sounds like it was a bad cry." Maybe I'm just supposed to make it better for the next bunch of women who come through. It does feel like more women who are moms are trying to negotiate that now. Me being quiet about it doesn't help anybody.

I'm very physical with color and sound. When I'm doing something right, I feel it in my whole body down to my feet. I think the volume doesn't hurt. I love being in a room with sixteen speakers and hitting the subs. It's gorgeous. That's the most fun I could have.

VIGNETTE 10

Kari, jewelry and album packaging designer, music lover:

Music has long been important to me. I am hooked on the collective experience of it: Everyone feels the same thing at the same time. Attending live shows. Being a part of something bigger. The live version is actually more like what the punk version of a song would be. Being a fan is a noble thing! Without fans, there would be no music scene. No one would sit and create and perform music in an echo chamber. Fandom is a noble profession. As the Mayhem girls have shifted into becoming parents, our music participation shifted to a life enhancer, instead of a lifestyle.

Becoming a mother—it was a big deal for me not to think about it and just think about art. And my thought was I would not become a mother. In 1995, we started doing juried craft shows. That's when I thought we're onto something. We've taken these techniques from more famous designers, and we're targeting the type of people who are into music and film.

I was convinced we were going to take over the world, and that jewelry would be the baby. And then Karen got pregnant. And I thought, "How are we going to conquer the world with a baby in tow?" Because it was very much me and Karen.

Tony, Dexter's dad, used to come into our store, Mayhem. He had leather pants from Leather Rose and he used to park his Harley out front. I don't think there was another person in the world who could have persuaded me to have a child with him. I had Dexter at forty. Tony and I had picked out all the birth music. The only band I remember was a friend of mine's band from Canada. By Divine Right, which is a nice idea, too: experiencing something that is about divinity, even though it's very earthly. I didn't want to forget it. For me, giving birth was like that scene in *American Werewolf in London* where the main guy's turning into the werewolf for the first time, and he's growing these claws, and his back is bending in all of these ways it's not supposed to. I was hoping later that Dexter was born during By Divine Right's song "Woke up in Birthday Suit." The birth was happy and funny and super fast. And I felt that at a certain point I didn't hear the music anymore.

Tony was right. It's been the greatest thing ever. Kids do give a lot of meaning to your life and they do add another perspective to your life, especially if you have a child who is different from you. I was working and mothering at the same time until Dexter was two years old. I got a clip-on Sassy seat for him, and he got into the flow of Mayhem. He was raised with adults and he was raised going to art parties.

But when I became a mother all of my creativity and ideas went away. It was about Dexter. They wouldn't come back. It was like the muse had left the building. And that was a big reason I was fine with letting Mayhem go. I wasn't creating. I wasn't getting great ideas. It was so strange. I spoke to one or two customers about it. And I asked an artist mom about it, and she corroborated this feeling: "Once I had my first child I lost all my ideas." I was shocked I wasn't an anomaly. It was hard. Like I said, jewelry was my baby, and now I have a real baby.

Now the ideas come more slowly and they're different. And I don't set aside time for it anymore.

VIGNETTE 11

Moan Elisa (music identity name), guitar player—The Trash Bags, stylist, store owner:

My dad was a maniac, an old biker, a wild man. I grew up at biker parties. All the bikes parked on the lawn. Real loose in the house, and so it follows, there was a lot of metal: Black Sabbath, Led Zeppelin.

But I really got into music when grunge came around, buying CDs and collecting posters. And then I started playing guitar around that time, too. My mom had an old acoustic guitar with nylon strings in the closet, and I started strumming it, and taking lessons with it. And soon, around twelve or thirteen, I was like, "I wanna plug in. I want an amp."

My first band was right around that time, too. A punk band at an all girls Catholic high school. We wore fishnets under our uniforms, creepers, and dog collars. That was in Orange County, which was a conservative area and that propelled us. Our band name was so embarrassing—Battlefield Nightmare. We recorded in my parents' garage. My mom eventually bought me an amp, and she would make me little bondage skirts.

After that, I stopped playing music for a very long time. I went to college, I started styling in Los Angeles, costuming bands for music videos. I was handed some major jobs out of the gate, and that was a sharp learning curve. Island/Sony/BMG would get a new band on the label, and I got to make bands look like bands. I dressed bands for Jay Leno and Jimmy Kimmel, and did some weird random jobs like picking up jewelry at Nikki Sixx's house.

I went to New York for my twenty-sixth birthday and met my future husband and bandmate Chuck Bones at Motor City Bar in the Lower East Side. I started going back and forth between Los Angeles and New York for a while, and then in 2008—the economy crashed. I was going from being double and triple booked to nothing. At that point, Chuck's partner had left, so Chuck and I made a little collection of t-shirts together, and Barnies in Japan picked up the first order. I thought, I should just move to New York and do this thing with Chuck. At first, our collaboration was called "Get Fucked, by Elisa and Chuck."

Two years into dating, I got pregnant with our first daughter, Johnnie Rose. That meant when we opened the store at 71 Orchard, we had a tiny baby with us. The shop was only 118 square feet, and I had her in an Ergo with a little crib in the corner, and people coming in and out all day. That was really hard. We were like, "What did we do?"

I bounced back really quick after the birth, but we're making this business, so it was a major challenge, and especially in New York too, with the logistics of it all and the stroller, and the snow and the rain, and the groceries, and the dog and laundry, and running a store all day every day. It was insane. I don't know how we did that. And then going out and going to shows and trying to have a life. And making new clothes. We were doing a lot—and I was still getting jobs styling in New York.

And then I thought, Johnnie needs a sister, and I totally made a girl happen—today's the day—let's go! It worked. I had Mickey Valentine at home in our tenement apartment, with a crazy thunderstorm. It was wild. She was a nine-pound baby with a midwife and doula. It was a really magical birth. But you know, still insane.

So Chuck and I had been talking about doing a band forever. But now we have two kids and a store. We were already a hub of activity, but I wanted to do it all again, as opposed to being behind the scenes. It was my push, my vision, and even though we had two babies, now ages three and one, I missed having a band.

It took a while to get the right combination of players together, but it finally clicked. Chuck's mom is in New Jersey, so she has been available to help with the kids, but she still works and is very active. She would watch them if we traveled somewhere to play or tour, but the majority of the time, it was the babysitters in the city. That was really hard, going to go play a show, and leaving the kids with sitters.

You go through this weird period where your body is literally taken over by someone else. You're in another frame of mind for a long time. I finally came back into my own body and my own self, and I remember thinking that I really need to do something for myself again. Being a mom is cool, but it's not who I really am. I did not see my own mom pursuing her passions. She was a housewife. She had three kids in the suburbs. Stayed at home. And that works for some people. But you're handed this lie: You're a mother. Now you're complete! I didn't want what my mother had. Many women wholly identify with that. And that's cool, too, but I've never felt like that. Being creative, being a stylist, being a designer for The Cast, opening my own store The Night Shift, playing music, it's all part of the same passion, and that's been behind the process of coming back into my own body and own sense of being.

And I love how our daughters are growing up. That they've had our stores, which are connected, to grow up in. We've always had parties in the store, and they've always had adults around, all these characters. Lots of cool people. I wish I had grown up like that. They're New Yorkers. Slash [from Guns 'n' Roses] came into the store once, and Johnnie was lying on the floor in the back of the shop with the iPad and Slash stepped over her and said, "What's your name?" And she told him, and he said, "I'm Slash." And she's like, "Whatever," and went back to what she'd been doing. And I'm like, do they know how significant all of this is? We brought them into this life and we brought that into their lives. When they were younger, I felt massive guilt: I didn't give them a comfortable house in the suburbs. They are not having "a regular upbringing," and now I see how cool they are. They're just so aware of things, and other people. They're open. I see it now, and I feel better about our choice.

To be honest, I still feel like a seventeen-year-old girl. I still feel very young. I never lost that. The rock 'n' roll bond. It's really specific to this little tribe on the Lower East Side. It's not just a phase in this community we have. Not a passing thing. It's really part of our identities. Our store on our Lower East Eide block really became this hub, keeping the pure rock 'n' roll flame alive. And the girls are growing up in that.

VIGNETTE 12

Nancy, makeup artist, music lover, former band member:

When I moved back from Germany to Los Angeles in 1979. I was sixteen and started getting into New Wave: Blondie, Talking Heads, B-52s. I started a trend in my high school of having a diagonal bang cut and I was a big Stevie Nicks fan, too. She was so free and witchy. I choreographed a dance to "Rhiannon" in high school, still a favorite song. I was kind of a music groupie before I knew what the word meant. I started dating these twins that were from this new wave band called St. Regis. I dated them one after the other, and then the drummer. I was twenty. I got into the metal scene around 1982. I was modeling, and met the bass player for the hair metal band Faster Pussycat, Eric Stacey. It was a crazy time. When I was dating Eric, I met Mötley Crüe at the Troubadour—where else?—in 1983. We called it "Troub-a-whore." Mötley Crüe were not big yet here, but they were big in Japan. They were wearing black leather and smelled so bad. Nikki Sixx was beautiful, but never showered. They were just down and dirty. Nice guys, though. There were lots of quaaludes being offered. I didn't want to take pills, but later on, I did love cocaine, which is crazy. My ex-fiancé, an engineer and producer, lived down the street from Steve Vai. So there were like little sugar bowls of cocaine all over his house and David Lee Roth was hanging out there. I did not get addicted, which was weird.

I was a dance major and was choreographing using music like the Residents and Black Flag, and in 1985, I was in a band called Pink, a funky, cool, New Wave band. And then a friend and I started a band called Aesthetica. Roxy Music with a hard edge. I was doing what Madonna did: I choreographed a whole thing with three dancers and we all sang backup with two lead singers. The '80s were so much fun in LA, but it was also crazy. My friends were starting to do heroin. I met my husband in 1991 in New York, and he kind of rescued me. I felt done with the music scene in LA and I really wanted to live in New York. My first apt in New York, we'd look down at Walter Cronkite having breakfast. And then I got married and lived with Don.

I never wanted to become a mother. I was into my own thing. I loved the life I had with Don. When I was thirty-eight, Don said, "Do you want to have a kid?" I looked at my imaginary wristwatch, and said, "Um. Okay." I figured I should do it. I didn't want to miss out on the opportunity. If I didn't, I think I would have regretted it. It was easy getting pregnant. I liked being pregnant, but I went through a really bad postpartum period that I didn't want medication for because I was nursing. I didn't do anything about it. I was just depressed, looking out the window thinking, I'll never be able to walk down the street again. It took me a long time to get used to being a mom. Then I found other mothers in the neighborhood.

When I thought about my life, I wanted to adventure and explore. At the last minute, I decided, "Well, this baby is another adventure. I have no idea, but let's do it. What's next?" I was ready for what's next. Music has influenced me for so much of my life, but now I just want silence most of the time. The sound of silence. I'm Art Garfunkel's makeup artist, by the way.

VIGNETTE 13

Mary, bass guitar—Jane Lee Hooker:

I met my husband Mark in 1993 in the East Village. He was in Wighat. He used to come see me play in the Wives—an all girl trio that I played bass in—before I even knew him. Then we started playing shows together, Wives and Wighat. East Village had such a great punk scene then. Ff, Lone Wolves, Mongrel

Bitch, Molotov Cocktail, so many great bands. Wives played Brownies, the Continental, CBGBs. In fact, Hilly Krystal, CBGB's founder, was our manager. We were on CBGB records, and CBs was our clubhouse. We played in the basement, and left our equipment in the basement. Hilly was such a creative, befuddled dude. I loved him so much. He was out of his mind. He really had vision. He put out our record, *Ripped*. We would go on our tour and he would give us his Suburban. We had a tour route we would take: down through the South, up to San Diego and then Seattle, diagonally down, Idaho, Topeka, Cheyenne. We opened for 7 Seconds, Blink 182—when they were just Blink. We played with the Mentors—they were so gross and mean. They called us "cunts" on the mic.

Mark and I got married in 1997. I was in my late twenties and I really wanted a baby. This chemical thing takes over. And I got pregnant and just kept playing. I was playing a show at CBs, and I'm wearing a big flannel and just walking around with a "bad back," so I couldn't lift anything. That was the last show we played. And we tell that kid now, "You were on stage at CBGBs, in utero!" I played until I was six months pregnant. Then something happened, where I was like, "This is fucked up, this is wrong." It was loud. Jack kicked a lot. It was mostly the volume. I felt like it was too loud for the baby. CB's fucking sound system. I really thought I was done. I put my bass up on the wall like it was art and it was just depressing. But I thought I was done, done, done, and didn't play for eight years or so. I thought I was too old, or this or that. Once Lucia was going to kindergarten, I thought, I have to figure something out. Because my husband started playing again, I started playing with my friend Sue and we were Futurex. Then I saw that Tracy started a blues band and Gita from Voluptuous Horror was her bass player. That gave me a pain in my chest. "Why didn't you ask me?" I asked her. So this is how Jane Lee Hooker came about.

I was super rusty, but it felt good. It still felt very secondary. Mommy-ing was very much first. Things started kicking into gear though. Jane Lee Hooker got signed, when I was playing with Future X, after going to rehearse after the kids' bedtime. It was very separate. I started with Jane Lee Hooker when Lucia was eleven, so you can see how big the gap was.

And then once the kids were adults, I just started incorporating them. Having Jack come on tour with me. And Lucia sells merch at every show. She actually sells the shit out of the merch. She's going to come with me on tour for a month.

I love being on stage. I'm very comfortable there, but put me in a Zoom meeting for work and I'm very silent. Being in a band—it's happiness, joy, and flow. Like skiing down a mountain, when you're fully in the present. That's what our shows are like now for me.

VIGNETTE 14

Darryl, artist, music lover:

When I was thirteen in Memphis, I found punk rock. Music and art saved my life. It was a really dark time for me. My parents were going through a divorce. There was abuse in the house. I was suicidal. I was struggling to find meaning and purpose. I was growing up in the Bible Belt, witnessing a lot of racism, personally experiencing anti-Semitism, and not really fitting in with the Jewish crowd either. And then I found Black Flag and Dead Kennedys albums.

I don't think having children was a huge dream of mine. I was twenty-four when I started going out with Scott. I saw his baby picture and it did something to me, and I thought, "I want to have a baby who looks like this." And I did! So there was something biological, but it was also about getting clean and sober, which I've been since age thirty.

I sang to my kids in utero. Happy songs. Kids' songs. Not punk rock, but I did attend a lot of shows when I was pregnant. There was a big Black Flag reunion show where all the different singers over the band's history took turns performing, and we were backstage in the VIP area with the bands. It was so glamorous and the music was so good. And I felt like my unborn child was getting that music. I felt like that would be good for kids to be there before birth.

After motherhood, I never thought I needed to take a break from my involvement with music. In fact when my kids were little, I'd dress them punk rock and take them to outdoor punk shows in Tompkins Square Park. I have all these adorable pictures of them there. Of course, as they got older they didn't want to participate with me anymore.

Motherhood feels basically the same now that I'm the age I am and long sober, except before I used to really want to meet the band and see what drugs they had and do drugs with them, and maybe have sex with them. (Laughs) And now it's more about the music. And sometimes I do want to meet them because of their art. I do feel something important when I go: Sometimes it's about feeling a release from my anxiety and pent-up anger. Sometimes it's about supporting a band's expressed politics. But it makes me feel high—like a natural high.

Attending live music now is more about the fact that I know it's going to be good for my soul. Maybe before it used to be more social, but now it's more about just hearing really good music—It's going to make me feel good. I need it, I feel like.

I go into the mosh pit less because I'm older and I'm more out of shape, and am more worried about getting hurt. But when I do get in the mosh pit, I love it. Being in the pit is an expression of anger and also freedom. I feel free. Just how you would dance, but to angry music. It feels really good.

Doing my own art and having my own life is a good example to set—I do have passions and have interests, lots of interests and a lot of them are political. My kids tend to be really impressed now, about the famous people I know, including musicians. They started wanting to wear some of my punk clothes, like my Fang hoodie. And my kid said, "I like the way it looks, but I'm not sure I want to wear it, because my friends might not know who they are." And I said, "Remember that the band stayed at our house?" When they wore it, their friends asked about it, and other kids were like "OMG, your mom's so cool!" They even asked my name and looked me up on Instagram and they were so impressed and it gave my kid some popularity—street cred! I think my kids never thought of me like that before and now they're starting to see me.

I love being a mother. I love every minute of it. I wanted kids. I loved kids. It made me so happy to be the kind of a mother that I wished I would have had. It came with me being clean and sober. When I was with kids, I couldn't be down. It was just fun. It's light.

I never used to think of myself as a fan, or a groupie. Music meant something to me and I felt a strong connection to it and the bands, and as I've gotten older, it makes sense that people take pictures of the bands when they go to shows. A lot of my friends were in the bands, and I wasn't, but it's a big part of me.

VIGNETTE 15

Tanya Hockley with Henk Suys, parents of Ruyter Suys, guitarist of Nashville Pussy:

Ruyter Suys, guitar player of the hard rock band Nashville Pussy, is our daughter. When she was little, she called us both "Mum"—she came up with it, and we were fine with it. Our generation was the first to question traditional parenting. We questioned everything. We made up our own rules. The '50s were so restrictive. Everything changed, and we got to help make the change.

Henk: I learned my guitar through folk music: Peter, Paul and Mary, the Kingston Trio.

Tanya: I was raised in northern British Columbia in the late '50s/early '60s when it was difficult to access a lot of music. But we had a local radio station where we heard most of the music. It was a lot of other things and a bit of jazz.

Tanya: I left home at seventeen, went right to the brand new university, Simon Fraser. There were no upperclassmen yet. I ended up just short of a degree in general studies. After I graduated from high school and went to Vancouver, when we went to rock concerts during university, everyone would be really quiet, and just listen. We really did form a musical identity, and really depended on the radio. FM stations had started, and they would play entire albums all at once. Every band wanted to be different. What was valued then was having candor. And we all tried to be kind to each other. That didn't last long.

Henk: Simon Fraser was the kind of place where you would see notices on the walls: "Anyone wanna do this thing?" There was a club for folk music, a club for creative writing. Tanya and I were in the same clubs. We were nineteen when we met. In 1967, we got pregnant. In 1968, Ruyter was born.

Tanya: I had already dropped out of university before I got pregnant. The pill had been invented but it was just for married women. It was unplanned—it freaked me out. I didn't want to be pregnant, but I was. It was pretty tough those first few months. We hadn't planned on being a permanent couple. We hadn't discussed that. Both of us had come from broken homes, so we were very determined to stay together and be a happy family. Henk was a hands-on dad, for the times. It was a hospital birth, and dads were just beginning to be in the delivery room. They weren't too crazy about him being there.

Henk: I needed to be there during the delivery. The messaging had been, "The men go over there." And I said, "No, I'm coming in." This was highly unusual. They made me cover my hair, which was long and curly. So I was allowed to be in, which was a wonderful experience.

Tanya: When I was about twenty-six or twenty-seven, I was in a choir that sang rock 'n' roll and folk songs, called Provisional Brass Tacks. We had a banner large enough to fit that name. I learned how to sing. Ruyter was there all the time. Everybody sang in those days. We had an excellent professional choir director, Doug Dodd, and I learned how to sing harmony. The choir was formed to train actors for musical theater productions.

Tanya: We lived in inexpensive, but interesting housing, and we were poor. But we didn't feel poor. We had friends, we had music. We ate health food. The daily bustle of things, coming and going. Someone bought us a diaper service. Ruyter never suffered. Our relatives were probably shaking their heads. This was the hippie lifestyle. Lots of friends and laughter. She was the first child born in that group of friends. Ruyter was raised by dozens and dozens of adults, all creative, who were really interested in her development. Ruyter would hold court. She was raised by a village and it shows.

Henk: One of the things about our house in downtown Vancouver was that it was built right next door to a rock concert hall, called various names, Dante's Inferno, The Retinal Circus: The Doors, Jefferson Airplane, Jimi Hendrix, Janis Joplin, they all came through town at some point. The Collectors were a fabulous band that played there. They didn't get very far. We generally assumed we were too broke to go in, but we didn't have to—we could hear through the wall. Ruyter must have heard that music from a cell, because it was always throbbing through the walls. It was a really big happening scene. Very creative and musical. There was a blues club in the basement called the Elegant Parlour that Jimi Hendrix played in quite a bit.

Tanya: I worked for an all volunteer-run radio station called CFRO. I was the producer of two children's dramatic shows and Ruyter was my main actor. She was so good. I also worked as a sound recorder at a nightclub every week for the radio. Once a week, we would go to a local nightclub called Rohan's and record from there for the station. There was a room upstairs with a tiny soundboard, and lots of dancing. It was before music became super, super loud, and it was really nice to have a club within walking distance.
Tanya: We introduced Ruyter to keyboard lessons at age three. These were Yamaha lessons and went for five years until she was eight. There she got excellent ear training. At eight, group lessons ended and she switched to one-on-one instruction, which she did not like. She locked herself in the bathroom when the instructor came for the lesson. That's when she switched to guitar, which is her current instrument in her current band. She played guitar all through high school. I'd had such a struggle with music and wanted it to be effortless for her.
Henk: I came into the relationship already being a guitar player and a folk singer. Ruyter was there watching what I was doing. As a teenager, Ruyter came up to me and said, "Dad, I can play that piece better than you." I was really shocked. I realized it was a moment in time where I could say one of two things. I said, "Yes, you can." I realized that was the right answer.

Tanya: Some of her own musical phrasing she can identify coming from Henk. Guitar saved Ruyter. She can fix guitars, and is really skilled. She had tough teenage years. It was tough on us. When she was fourteen, she turned into somebody else. She was getting into heavy metal. Metallica was her favorite band of that time. And Slayer. I remember overhearing her listening to Slayer and thinking, What is this? This is awful. She told me it was a Christian heavy metal band. She was finding her own music, apart from ours. But rock is 100 percent the reason for her not having kids of her own. The constant touring. I don't know how she does it. I went on tour with her band, Nashville Pussy, for two weeks. Every night the same energy. Soundcheck, eat, perform, stay up until 4 a.m. and then sleep and get up and repeat. It was awkward being the mom. I felt like the old woman on the bus, but I went on tour with them in Europe. I hadn't been to Europe before, and we went to fabulous cities. In Madrid, the band was at soundcheck, and I was just wandering through the streets by myself looking for the club where Ruyter would play that night. There weren't even posters advertising the band. And I couldn't find it. I knew the name of the club: Club del Sol. So I'm wandering all day long, and then I see a man wearing a Nashville Pussy t-shirt. I went up to him and grabbed his shirt and pointed to the image of Ruyter on it and said, "Me Mama!" and he spoke English. He didn't even know the band was playing. I got him two comps for the show. To be a mum of a band like that, to be Ruyter's parents, that is exciting.

VIGNETTE 16

Jessica, music journalist and critic, author, director/producer of *Women Who Rock* documentary series:

At twelve or thirteen, I was into the B-52s, Neneh Cherry, Deee-Lite, and Sinead O'Connor, who I was obsessed with. But I didn't so strongly identify with this music in a way that I did once I found punk a few years later. I look back now and these artists foreground that I was looking for the "punk rock" in things. When my friend Andrew Semens gave me a punk rock mixtape at fifteen, I jumped headfirst into it immediately. It was definitely the more artful side of punk: Pussy Galore, the Boredoms, Big Black, this weird survey. Very immediately I was like, this is my whole thing. It was weird to go from Deee-Lite to Pussy Galore. But it was a balm. Like a piece fitting into place. I was hungry for this loud, wild thing. And then when I saw girls in bands, women in bands, like Babes in Toyland and Bikini Kill, who I saw on their first US tour, I wanted to be just like these women, and I started to piece some of that together. First, a wardrobe initially, and then kind of an attitude and identity. I lived in Minneapolis when I saw Bikini Kill. They were really scary, but really exciting, and were my introduction to punk feminism. Two days later, I managed to cobble together everything I saw Kathleen Hanna wearing on stage, including garters over tights. (Where would I have gotten a garter belt that would have fit me?) And a kilt I wore every day. I was naturally misandrist. I really hated men. I really didn't like boys. I just thought women and girls were so much cooler and that men were the evildoers of the universe. They were the ones who were killing the earth and being gross war-mongering presidents. At the same time, I was very aware of the low expectations for me as a girl in every way, at shows, in school, on the street. I was very much already a young activist. I didn't go to camps in the summer. I would go and volunteer at non-profits near my house: NARAL or NOW, the Committee for Latin America. I was in sixth grade, the same age as my son. I would go to rallies and lay down on the freeway on ramp to get the United States out of whatever. Or impeach Dan Quayle. What happened to that shirt? Going out getting signatures with a twenty-eight-year-old activist. Running into my stepdad when I was wearing a gas mask. That was my whole deal. I spoke at protests about a parental consent law for abortion in the late '80s. I got asked to speak at a pro-choice rally when I was twelve or thirteen, and I took two buses there.

But once I found punk feminism which was personal, I thought, "This is my war zone now, and not just my cool hobby." It gave a way to tie parts of me together: one that believed in music and the one that really wanted there to be a different and just world. A couple of days after high school, I moved myself to LA and started working at a very low level in the music industry. I started my own business when I was nineteen doing public relations. I thought I was going to be a photographer, but all my cameras got stolen. I thought I might be a roadie. I didn't have a big plan, but I knew what I was good at and I knew I wanted to be around music. I think I was too excitable and midwestern and earnest for LA, but I joined a band. And as a PR person, I worked with independent bands and record labels. I worked with Trenchmouth, whose drummer was Fred Armisen, future *SNL* cast member. I did a fanzine, *Hit It or Quit It*. I started my fanzine in the pre-Riot Grrrl era when I was fifteen and the last issue came out when I was twenty-eight or twenty-nine. People still talk to me about it. A lot of people got their start writing for *Hit It or Quit It*. The pop critics for *The New York Times* and the *Washington Post* were both *Hit It or Quit It* writers. In 1996, at age twenty, I moved to Chicago.

I did have a band in LA, though. We had a boy who sang and played guitar, and someone said, "It's weird you have a band with girls, but the girls don't sing," and I said, "That's kind of the whole point." By that point, I'd been playing really poorly for four or five years. I was serious about being in my band. It was all I had to do. At the tail end of my twenties, I toured nationally and internationally with bands. A band called Challenger. I played drums in a band on Kill Rock Stars. I loved playing, towards the end of the tours it was quite transcendent, but being on stage was hard. A lot of the main tour, we were second on a five-band bill, and I was the only girl. It was like twenty-seven guys and me. I felt like a total alien. It was like being spiritually hungry all the time. I would run into a girlfriend or a woman in another band and we'd just gravitate towards each other.

I've been diagnosed with PTSD from working in the music industry and working in music journalism and playing in bands. Literally, it says in my medical report that it's a cumulative result of twenty years of enduring sexism, hostility, misogyny, and sexual harassment. But I absolutely think that's par for the course for women who stick around in music. It is unavoidable. So many of the older women artists I've interviewed have just been resigned to it: "That's just how it was." It was like you had to have a boyfriend in the business or you were just in for it. Because I was a publicist, I had a lot of proximity to powerful men and because I was a good publicist, people wanted to stay in my favor. I think sometimes that protected me a little bit, but it did not keep me from harm. It did not keep me from trauma. Playing in a band, I experienced being catcalled on stage. I experienced the sexism of low expectations in every show. People were surprised I could actually play. They were really surprised I wasn't dating a member of the band. They were surprised I'd been in bands previously. Being surprised I knew anything technical. Being surprised I was even there. My bandmates made fun of me for wearing jewelry and makeup. There was a different kind of pressure. Even though I wasn't the singer in the band, people were staring at me. I was the girl, the thing. The bauble. And because I was on the road with all these boys, sometimes they wanted to tell me their problems and be like their little therapist. And I was like, "No. There's twenty-seven of you, like literally fuck off."

I did think about motherhood around this time. I was about twenty-seven. I had a boyfriend who was a fairly famous rapper. And he already had a kid and he really wanted to have more kids. I hadn't thought much about kids before, because I was so focused on my career. But also I'd had some boyfriends who were all very active in their alcoholism and drug addiction, and I thought I wouldn't want to replicate this person's gene pool. My boyfriend, the rapper with the kid, said, "We can't have kids unless you write at least one book. Otherwise, you're never going to get it done." So that was in my mind. Very fortunately, we broke up soon after. Around the time I was twenty-eight or so, I was thinking seriously about it. I think there was something hormonal. I began thinking that there's got to be something bigger than my career, something more than the effervescence of this lifestyle. But if I'm going to be a mom, I need to make space in my life now for this. I'm going to do what I can to adapt my life to work less and have this other space that's not "workspace." I don't know where I came up with this: that I needed to figure out how to make my living from twenty hours of work per week, because I thought that's how much a mom could work, maybe. And so I started moving towards that when I was about twenty-eight, which was great. It allowed me to push towards making a little bit more money. I had been on tour and gone to Japan, and then I got a book deal and so I knew I was making that space. But I also didn't know at the time who I was going to have kids with, but I still made that space. The person who is now my husband literally came into my life around that time. He'd been in a band that I'd worked with. We had known each other for about a decade. Then we got engaged and a few months later we were pregnant. And that was right as my first book tour ended. All right in a row. I had our son William when I was thirty-two.

When I was five months pregnant with William, I went and covered SXSW in Austin. I was coming from a show and some drunk frat bros got really close and pretended like they were going to punch me in the stomach. And I was so scared and I started having a panic attack and went back to my hotel room and stayed there for like two days and didn't finish reporting anything. The last time I deejayed, I was seven-and-a-half months pregnant and being in the club and trying to navigate that space as someone who needed to protect that space around her body, I thought I can't do this again. It was so dark, people couldn't see me, and I felt vulnerable and needed to have that space. Then I was tired and didn't want to go to shows as much and was really sick during both my pregnancies. I actually went into labor at Pitchfork Festival when Robyn was playing and I hated being in that space as a pregnant person, my incubator phase of being a mom, because it was all these twenty-something guys, saying, "You look like you're about to pop!" And then when I had William, six-and-a-half weeks early, of course I wasn't going to shows. But what I was doing for a living was covering local music, and my husband and I were living on my freelance salary, and I couldn't say no to things. But there were certain things I just couldn't cover anymore because I had an infant and was breastfeeding. I couldn't pump enough to be gone for longer than a couple of hours, and even if I could, was I going to pump at the interview? I still have a resentment against Mike Watt [from the Minutemen], who wouldn't stop talking during our interview. I told him, "Listen, I have to go," and I got mastitis from being delayed from pumping, because he wouldn't stop.

I was the first mother to work at Pitchfork when they'd been a website and a cultural force for nineteen years. The practical aspect of being involved in music was having to keep up the appearance for all the editors I work with, mostly men. In other words, I had to minimize the hassle of motherhood, so that I could remain employable. Even just two or three years ago, a woman editor who didn't have children asked me, "Don't you have to talk to your husband before you commit to this story? For traveling?" And I responded, "No, I'm literally the breadwinner in my family. We have babysitters. I can leave." Part of it was about making sure I was seen being out. I had to go to things/shows early on, to prove I could still go to shows, like covering Pitchfork one year before I worked there. I went at that time because it was still a big networking thing. And I wasn't in a position to turn work down so I didn't, and I didn't want to be the new mom who couldn't file in time. My second son, Jude, was four months old and I pumped at that festival and I had a backpack with my ice bag in there, and was jokingly showing it to my friends who worked at *The New York Times*: "Covering the festival for me is different for me than it is for you." I was literally trying to find someplace to pump at an outdoor festival backstage. I pumped in Porta Potties at Lollapalooza, which was probably deeply unhygienic, but I was pumping to just pump. And I started to see and understand really quickly why there weren't more moms in music. Why were they such a rarity? I only knew one other woman in music criticism who had a child, Marissa Moss, who has two. I knew some women who had bands. Lots of times they were married to their band partners. And I still know almost no mothers in music with more than one kid. So it was going to shows, it was keeping up with things—or having the appearance of keeping up with things, and going out and being seen, even if it was just literally putting in an appearance, so that one of my bosses, or editors would see me at a show. But what I wrote about and how I wrote about it became different. I was no longer doing live show reviews—things where I'd have to stay up until 2:30 in the morning to file. That went away until my kids were quite a bit older. So I took other assignments that were beneath me because they allowed me to be home, and not have to hire a babysitter. The very quiet thing that I understood from canonical rock misogyny is that motherhood is antithetical to rock music. Anything that had to do with moms was uncool. People were like, "How dare you bring your baby on that road." People would be like, "Okay, I'm dropping out because I'm a mom now. "Oh, that's like Mom music." "That's what moms listen to." It was a pejorative. A put down. That was also the big insult with Lilith Fair. It was a place for "moms to go" and sit on their picnic blankets with their kids, a place that was safe because "moms value safety." So then punk rock or rock spaces are not places for mothers. I missed shows and I missed relating to people on that level. It became very clear which of our friends were going to visit us or be willing to hang outside of a bar setting. It shaved off lots of people. When we had our first kid, I qualified for public aid. I had my first child and it was paid for by the state, because I was so broke. Motherhood gave me a different kind of ambition because I couldn't be "pre-kid era broke" and have a kid. I got a lot more serious about not letting anything stand in my way, like interviewing Willie Nelson during my newborn's naptime and going, "I have twenty-five minutes with him on the phone at best." I would nurse my infant while I was doing phone interviews and just talk really quietly because then I could ensure there wouldn't be a screaming baby. I tried to minimize, as much as possible, anyone's knowledge of me being a mother. It was regarded as unprofessional and uncool. When I would go out, people would ask, "Where's your kids?" Well, I just locked them in the garage.

I think in the last couple of years, things have changed a little bit, with pop stars who have such an immense reach. The ascendancy of certain pop artists, be it Beyonce or Brandi Carlisle, or different people who have made motherhood a piece of their art and do not obscure it at all. I think these artists have made motherhood artful to the populace, and I think that makes motherhood cooler. Like Beyonce in her super pregnant kind of regalia or her sister, Solange, or Cardi B. These images, I think, have exploded the idea of what a rock mother can be. And I also think about the mothers of the '70s. Laura Nyro and Patti LaBelle briefly raised their kids together when they were both single moms. That wasn't well publicized at all. It's much harder to think about anyone who made motherhood a feature of their career, because it was just such a liability then. I think the things people think the least about, or are the least conscious about, is motherhood and ageism. Even the way that they fit together. If you're old enough to have a baby, then you're going to retire or you should retire. Separately, I think women in music face ageism earlier and much more significantly than men do. Nothing like making this documentary with a bunch of women who are over fifty, over sixty, even over seventy and some over eighty to really drill that home, whether they want to talk about it or not. It comes up even when hearing from press people, who regard my documentary content as "retro." It's Shania-fucking-Twain, dude. When is she not relevant? But you know, in the same breath, they are covering the fucking Rolling Stones documentaries that are coming out. Those guys are older and they suck now. Sometimes I see it in peoples' socials and writing. I'll comment and be like, "What you're saying here is that mothers do not belong in this space," and I think that's really ignorant, and then people like Björk, too, have never shied away from making music about motherhood, and is also one of those people who maybe makes it possible to be a true artist and a mother. I think people think that's not reconcilable. Because to be a true mother, you have to be completely giving. And to be a true artist, you have to shut out everyone's needs but your own.

We had a brief few months where both Matt and I had busy careers, and it just felt like our family was going to atomize. In general, we have no time together. My joke is that he's the day manager and I'm the night manager. Without really trying, every two years one of us would be the one who had a career. Then when my book blew up and my career really took off, and I got a job at *MTV News* and was traveling so much, Matt, who was a lawyer, worked a little, but was a full-time dad. I told him basically that I had to go prove myself while I could, while there was all this momentum, before age, womanhood and motherhood caught up with me. I didn't know if I'd have these jobs if I wasn't all in. I wanted to show people what I could do, so I could continue to be at least moderately expensive in the future. Once our kids were in grade school, I had a job at Spotify where I had to travel a lot more than they told me, and I felt like I couldn't say anything if I wanted to be taken seriously. I was the only one at Spotify who had two jobs. I edited the print magazine and then I also worked on the website daily. I had my own vertical which was doing gangbusters, so I worked a lot at night after my kids went to bed. And I had to leave at 4:30 p.m. every day to get my kids. All the dads there would stay late. They'd go out drinking, go to shows. I'd been getting all my work done from home because my kids had pink eye back-to-back-to-back. When I returned my boss said, "That's your vacation time." There were a handful of people around us in the office. My boss started taking a poll amongst them. Was it fair that Jessica gets to work from home? One woman said, "That's not my problem, I hate children." The other friend who was a parent was just looking at me stricken. Then these bros in sales thought they should be able to work from home, too. I pointed out that I start back at work every night at 8:30 or 9:00 p.m. and work until 1:00 or 2:00 a.m., so I'm basically working at least twenty hours outside at work. And I started crying. He was like, "You shouldn't be working that much! The next day, they moved me into an office entirely by myself. I was the only person then who had the office with a door so I couldn't talk to anyone. That's what it's like to be in spaces that have never had a mom in them.

There's been times when amid a book tour and when I worked at *MTV News*—I was gone for six straight weeks once. Once I got back, it took weeks to become a part of the dynamic of the house again, to have any authority. When Covid happened, I had two years where everything just drifted away, because all there was was care. For mothers, balance is a farce. I interviewed Macy Gray for a show about being a mother. And she said, "There's no such thing as balance. You just do it and you just barrel on, because if you stop to think about it and how you're doing it, you'll fucking shoot yourself." If Macy Gray, who's sold like 21 million copies of her record, is telling me this, I can't even consider how life might work if I just did this, or if I just got a big book advance to pay for an au pair. I interviewed Rickie Lee Jones. She said, "Once you become a mother and you get that third eye, it might move around your head but it doesn't leave. That third eye is always looking out or thinking about the wellbeing of the child." I'm very fortunate to be at a place where I'm getting offered bigger opportunities when literally I thought I'd be done having a career by the time my kids were this age. I didn't see a model. Now, I do more directing in the world of television and film, as there are more women of a certain age still working in that industry.

So the documentary series *Women Who Rock* had been developed by a group of men who had worked on a documentary punk series. They had come up with this idea and there had been different thoughts of who would produce it. Covid stalled it. Finally, they Googled "woman rock critic" and found me and Ann Powers. It was a complete surprise. They were looking for a writer to map the whole thing. They didn't have a director. I was suggesting people, but I also told them that I've produced and directed stuff before. And then they called me and offered it to me to direct and executive produce and so this is what I'm going to do now.

I think about Patti Smith, breaking out big as a rock artist in 1975, and how interesting it is that six years after, she moves to Michigan for marriage and motherhood, and is by any definition essentially a suburban housewife. I think about this during the summers, now that I'm able to have space of "not work" sometimes, that when I just "be a mother" and just do "mother things," I feel like I'm a Lego that's plopped into this thing where everything works. Because the most disruptive thing a mother can have is any ambition outside of herself and especially when mothers are doing something that's trying to speak to the wider world or broader audience. The less need I have to express myself or be like a full human being, the easier it is to be a mom. When I have space and time to just be a mother, it's much simpler. It's not intellectual. About as intellectual as it gets is reading beside the community pool or the beach. Mothering is a spiritual exercise. It is nature. And I see how much my children thrive with my full attention. When I have a lot of demands on my professional or artistic self, I find it very difficult to be as present, and there's a lot of things that just don't run right in our house. This is my year of trying to undercompensate. There's just a lot of things around my house that I've just stopped doing. Does this actually fall apart? I'm interrogating it all.

VIGNETTE 17

Dana E., costume designer:

I've always identified with alternative culture. I was a teenager in the '70s. I read *Steal This Book* by Abbie Hoffman. My father was a special investigator for the FBI, but I hung out with all these renegades. For me, it was music, boys, clothes. I made my own clothes. This was South Carolina in the early-to-mid '70s. There was no Internet. There was no Hot Topic. If you wanted to dress alternatively, it was DIY. I taught myself to sew. I made clothes that I copied off of Sly and the Family Stone album covers. I went to thrift stores and dressed like Janis Joplin. I cut off vintage velvet dresses into mini dresses, put feathers in my hair and was a bit of a wild child. Or I wanted to think I was. I presented that way for sure. It was not normal to identify this way in my small town of Greenville in the mid-70s. It was divided, freaks, frats, geeks. I was definitely a freak. Music was always important. It spoke for the counterculture. I was a peacenik, hippie-ish type of person. Then in the late '70s, I went to Columbia, South Carolina, ostensibly to go to college and joined a commune, and a food co-op and dropped out of college and started traveling. This was a place of blue laws. They roll up the sidewalks on Sunday. Very churchy. The hippies and the freaks really stood out there. I got the opportunity to travel across the country, and ended up in Portland, Oregon, where I was part of a theater troupe. Punk rock was starting to make itself known. Elvis Costello, reggae. I began to relate to that. I came back to South Carolina and blew all the hippies away, because all of a sudden I was a punk rocker. I had the hightop "Cons" and the fur coat. Because I was a costume designer, it was important to me to embellish myself, and important to me to listen to certain kinds of music. So to express my allegiance to my views, it was important to embellish myself.

    I graduated high school when I was sixteen, essentially because I could read, they wanted me out of there. I was a rabble rouser in high school. At this time, it was the ending of the peaceniks, and the beginning of the nihilism of punk rock. And I, sadly, especially related to that. Until I became a mother, to jump ahead. Once you become a mother, someone else is in front of you. It's not as much about you anymore. I moved to New Orleans in 1978. That opened up another entire world of music for me, because of the heavy influence of Afro-Caribbean music, R&B, and soul. I got a job at Tipitina's as a bartender and worked in the kitchen. I was the little punk rock chick in the kitchen. So I was not only listening to this music, but actually meeting artists like Professor Longhair, James Booker, Roosevelt Sykes, Fats Domino, Earl King, the Neville Brothers were the house band, and the punk scene was in stride there. All kinds of new wave and art bands and I was right smack dab in the middle of the shit. I could not have been happier. It was a gift. It was magical. That propelled me forward and rounded out my education.

    It was at Tipitina's that I met my future ex-husband. At one point, we decided to go to Europe, and at that time, you flew out of New York. We stayed with a friend. Remember, I was raised in South Carolina, a reasonably provincial girl. Going to the West Coast opened my brain, moving to New Orleans opened my brain. Going to Europe widened everything. When we got back to the States and were about to return to New Orleans, a friend of ours had an apartment in the East Village. And without further ado, we packed up and moved to the East Village. That was the Dharma Bum mentality. I felt like I had outgrown the scene in New Orleans. I was looking to broaden my horizons, and was enamored of the gritty, dirty New York scene, and an opportunity presented itself. It was 1982 and the neighborhood was pretty wild, pretty dangerous, eye opening. I found myself pregnant in the middle of this scene. Cabs wouldn't take me to my building on Avenue B. We decided to get married. Our marriage lasted a little over a year. I was very young. I was twenty-five. In the East Village, there was maybe one other pregnant girl who I knew at the time. Two pregnant punks. I was relating to the art, the scene, the music. I kept that identity even when I became pregnant and after my child was born. I was still living an alternative lifestyle. I had Della in a natural childbirth clinic on the Upper East Side. I didn't want to be all drugged up. I gave birth, and I was home the next day in my squalid East Village tenement. Not long after, I split up with her father, and he kept the apartment for whatever reason. In hindsight, it shouldn't have been that way, but I was anxious to get out of the situation and was a fairly headstrong child with a child, as they say. I skated around with friends, but that also happened to be the beginning of the real estate boom in Manhattan. All of a sudden, there were no apartments to be had. I was a single mom, working in a bar with a baby. The situation was untenable. Reality hit. I had a baby. I had a bartending job and no place to live. I ended up moving to Greenpoint in 1985. So I was with a little baby on the L train, walking through an abandoned shithole to get to my shithole basement apartment. Greenpoint and Williamsburg as we know it didn't exist then. It was fairly desolate, a little bit frightening, and I was chugging along. One day it was February, I had Della in the stroller on Avenue C and I was looking at this abandoned building where people were squatting, and wondered if I could get in on some squat situation, and I looked down at my little girl in the stroller in the snow and thought, What the fuck am I doing?

I pulled my head out of my ass and moved back to New Orleans, where I had friends who had kids, there was grass, she could run around in the yard. I feel strongly that I made the right move to come back to New Orleans, still rife with music and culture. I did really well for myself here. Back then if you had an ounce of motivation in the Big Easy, you could run circles around everyone else. And that's what I did, apparently. My daughter is grown and she has two kids, so now I'm a grandmother, which is awesome. I still have my opinions, my political beliefs, my music, and my punk rock haircut. And when I became a mother, it was more important for me to hang on to that identity. I was twenty-five. I had no fucking clue what I was doing being a mom. Even under the best of circumstances, there's nothing that can really prepare you for motherhood. You just kind of wing it. Your body changes, your chemistry changes, your brain changes, but still, Della and I grew up together, because I was kind of clueless. The shock of being responsible for someone else hit me pretty hard. I loved and still love being a mother, I love being a grandmother. I can be a rock 'n' roll granny now. It's an integral part of my identity, but it has always been important for me to retain myself. That can be a struggle. When Della was younger, she may have been a little embarrassed of me. Maybe she wanted a little more normalcy than I had to give as a single working mom in the film business. She said something about my leather jacket or something. I said, "Look honey, I love you, but just because I got pregnant, I'm not going to be a casserole mom. This is me. You're you. We're going to make this work. I'm figuring it out as I go. I'm going to make mistakes. I'm trying to have everything be in your best interest, however, I'm still going to henna my hair. So suck it up, kid!" She sucked all of the beauty and brains from me coming down the birth canal. She's accomplished, has a great job. She's smart as a whip. She's artistic. She's beautiful. She's all the things and more that I hoped she could be. I'm sure I did some damage. All mothers do, without even trying. We still call each other at least every other day. We hang out together. It's good.

VIGNETTE 18

Helixx C. Armageddon (music identity name) lyricist, vocalist, performance artist, experimental music producer:

I just released an album entitled *House of Helixx*. Helixx C. Armageddon is the name that I create all of my art under. It is the name I go through much of the world with. I've had this name since I was fourteen. How I chose the name "Helixx" comes from the fact that I'm a lyricist. My style was molded through hip hop. People would say when I was first coming up, you flow, you sound like you're infinitely flowing. The helix DNA strand infinitely flows. That became my first name. I wanted a name that was ambiguous: a universal name that didn't sit in any specific space. You don't know who or what I am. I'm part of everyone like the DNA strand. C is the Roman numeral for one hundred. And Armageddon? Warlike times. So my name means "infinitely flowing 100 percent through warlike times." My fourteen-year-old self thought, "I'm going to give myself a first name, a middle initial, and a last name," because there might be fifty other artists who call themselves Helixx. That fourteen-year-old vision was correct. There is no other Helixx C. Armageddon.

I was raised in South Jamaica, Queens, which during the '80s was a pretty tough neighborhood. I also grew up in a very diverse family of African, Italian, and Caribbean cultures. My grandmother played country music. My grandfather played a lot of jazz. My parents played '70s soul. My dad played reggae. "Playing" meant records and radio. Country and soul music started my love affair with story. Country music had such great stories. I remember tuning into the music and listening to the words. For me, my connection to music has always been about the words and how I get pulled into the sonic story. My uncles, who were also in the house, listened to punk, hip hop and what was popular on the radio at the time. There was such a diverse soundscape when I was growing up in my home. It was very different from what my friends were experiencing in their homes, where they only listened to one thing. This whole demographic array became a soup for my brain. I was taking it all in. I was always most attracted to music that took all of me and made me feel something in a dramatic way. Because my uncles were ten to twenty years older than me, I had punk and hip hop coming in. And my parents were pretty young—they had me in their early twenties. I remember loving certain songs. And I remember if I wanted to feel a certain thing, there was certain music I gravitated towards.

I loved Black Sabbath at the time. I loved Nirvana. Hip hop called to me on so many different levels because of its stories. There was Salt-n-Pepa and there was Rakim. Within country music there was Kenny Rogers, his song "The Gambler" was one of my all time favorite songs. When it came on, I thought "There's something tough that's about to happen that I don't want to be present for, but I definitely wanted to hear about it." So that was the start of the musical adventure, and the place I turned to for everything. My mom was a poet/writer. I was the youngest in our working class house, where at one point, there may have been ten or eleven people living in it. There weren't televisions all around, and as the youngest, I had no rank on what was available to watch. But I did have my own radio. I grew up on horror films. My parents are huge horror buffs. I was very much from a home that was fueled by horror films. Stylistically, that has influenced how I present myself in the world. Whenever I needed to escape the dramas of the house, I would go to my room with my radio. Many people grow up in challenging homes, where there may be toxicity or violence. For me, music was a place I could go. It was a safe place and I could be transported to another realm. It was almost like my version of an imaginary friend because the songwriters seemed to understand what I was experiencing. They told a story I couldn't tell. When I was fourteen, I got my first job at a flea market on 4th and Broadway next to Tower Records. All throughout high school, I worked there, selling vintage clothes and getting exposed to the wonders of downtown New York City, and its live music scene. The Nuyorican Poets Cafe didn't check for IDs, so after I finished work, there might be a show and my friends and I could go there. Or Bowery Poetry Club. And CBGB on a good night, when the door was being cool. These places also gave us a place to perform in.

I started performing around fifteen, and Nuyorican was one of the places that invited me in. Downtown was so wonderful during the '90s, being a young person, experiencing everything about St. Mark's Place, and Trash and Vaudeville, which is where I got many of my style influences. I wore a lot of vintage clothes back then, too, and inside the thrift stores you had access to vinyl and cassette tapes. There was constant exposure to music, then I became a part of hip hop by performing. Around the age of fourteen, I co-founded the gender justice collective called The Anomolies. I fell in love with hip hop during what is often called its golden age, which included artists such as Public Enemy, Rakim, Tribe Called Quest, Queen Latifah, Slick Rick, MC Lyte, Salt-N-Pepa. Later, Nas, Wu-Tang Clan, Jay Z and so many other individuals brought it into the mainstream. The Anomolies would do hip hop performances in a lot of DIY spaces all around Manhattan. And then we started to travel and tour. I was experiencing all of the elements of hip hop culture, which included graffiti, DJing, MCing, and Breakin.' I always loved feeling like I was in on the best kept secret, because these downtown venues made you feel like you were going into a portal leading to something special. For me, it's the same feeling I get when I perform and I go into flow. When everything feels in mystical alignment: the music, the energy in the room, the people, the soundscape, who you are in that moment and how everything comes together. It's one of the ways I can have a transcendental experience. Coming through music in '90s-era downtown New York City, in all those different music spaces, I was able to have those moments.

It was during the early 2000s that I started venturing to concerts. This is when I really got into symphonic metal. One of my friends exposed me to the music: Epica, Nightwish, Opeth, Children of Bodom. Dream Theater is one of my favorite bands of all time. I got a chance to go to one of their last shows with Mike Portnoy, who was their incredible drummer. Those experiences were very influential on me from a storytelling perspective. One of my favorite songs is "Chasing the Dragon" by Epica. The way the song is put together is beautiful, and the storytelling with sound is all encompassing. The vocal tone and the amount of space in the music for reflection was always striking to me. The first time I experienced this was with Opeth, during a song that played for more than ten minutes. It's not uncommon in symphonic metal to have no lyrics for five minutes and just pure soundscape. Very different from hip hop. You generally don't have long gaps of instrumental reflection in hip hop. For me, when I was going to see symphonic metal bands play, I was enamored by the use of space in song, and how it would drive you somewhere. It could drive you to be angry. It took you on a journey with no words, just soundscape. Another group that I listened to during that time was Metallica. They were one of my all time favorite bands, again because of storytelling. *Unforgiven I* and *II*. Those songs were my heart. Another group I listened to was Mastodon. Their song "Show Yourself" was my "get ready to go out" music. With that said, music has been the foundation of healing, friendship, community, and connection. Through the subcultures I've participated in including the downtown club scene, I've met most of my friends. The music called to all of us, and we ended up in those spaces. For me, that is an organic byproduct of participating in music culture. It calls similar beings into the same places of engagement. You feel like you're part of something greater than yourself.

At around nineteen, I worked for Upstairs Records, an international mail order company in New York. They supplied records, lighting and deejay equipment in the late '90s, and that's where I met my son's father. We essentially met at a record company, on the distribution side. I remember learning I was pregnant in the bathroom stall of a venue. The bathroom door was broken, and I had one boot on the door, holding it shut. I was having this moment because I felt different. I was doing the math in my head. And I thought, Am I pregnant? And I was. And outside the bathroom, the music's loud, and someone's trying to get in. But I was having this moment of clarity: I'm pregnant. I know it. I had just gotten off stage from performing, and I was hit with a wave of nausea. The song I was performing was called "Blacklisted." Me and Jise One from the Arsonists were just spotlighted in *Time* magazine for this song. Back then, *Time* was an important magazine, and we were performing after the article broke. At that point, I was three months pregnant. I continued to do performances until my brain said, this is not healthy. What wasn't healthy was the smoked out spaces I was performing in, and the nature of live shows. But I continued up until right around the seventh month. And I didn't take a tour, which is one of the things I still think about. I was approaching eight months, and I was asked to go perform in Paris. I was on a record that was released through Toy's Factory, one of Japan's top four record labels. My doctor said, "I'm not flying out to deliver your kid in Paris. I can't guarantee that with the cabin pressure that you won't deliver early." One of my collective mates went in my place and did my verses.

I got signed during the time I was pregnant. It was good timing to be signed to a record label that had a bigger distribution. But the challenge of the time was around Napster, and the consolidation of all the big record companies. And I was still in development so didn't move forward with the other artists that were further along. I was young. I was filled with all these emotions of pregnancy, then I got signed, and when you get signed, you start down a path that you assume will be a world-bending experience, and then you get shelved, so that experience isn't realized. But in my case, I had this baby that's about to be born. So it was a weird time, and so much of music was changing during that time, too. Because of the introduction of streaming, first illegally and then legally, the music industry was trying to figure out who they were. Being a young artist at that time, I was also trying to figure out who I was, which we all do for the rest of our lives. But at the time, I didn't realize that. And we're still coming into awareness. You just add different layers of life to that same narrative. You keep adding rings to your story like a tree. At the core, you're still that emo kid that you were. You're still the person, but evolved.

I had my son in 2000. I gave birth when I was twenty-one. My son's very first concert was Immortal Technique, who is a fantastic hip hop artist. His first arena concert was KISS at Madison Square Garden. I was like if we're going to start anywhere with concerts, let's break the pyrotechnics out. He was probably five. He was raised on St. Mark's Place in the East Village, because when I was fourteen, I remember walking down St. Mark's Place with a skateboard on my back, thinking if I ever have a kid, this is where he's going to grow up, and I made that happen. My son's father and I never married, but stayed together for several years. I've raised my son as a single mom with heavy support from my family. He's a good young adult. But those years were tough. Being a single parent is tough in general, being how New York City is. If you're here and raising a child and you are alone, it is a very tough city: The time constraints of work, and having an art practice and trying to raise a kid. I had to make a choice back then. I decided I wanted to raise him in a space that was open, where he could be creative. The same things I fell in love with as a kid when I came to the city, the same things that attracted me to downtown, I wanted to give that experience to him. But in order to give him that, I knew that I couldn't have it all during these years. I had to focus on being present as a mom and focus on keeping a stable home. I had been a couch-surfing artist. When he was in high school, I said, "When you're in college, I get to go back to the couch-surfing artist I always wanted to be." But when he was young, I intentionally took a step back to be there fully during the formative years. If I set him up with a solid foundation, he would have the tools he needed to survive.

Motherhood is definitely an identity. You see so much of the world through the eyes of motherhood. For me, it has developed and expanded perspective, and keeps me in touch with the fact I am part of an ecosystem. There is a level of awareness that motherhood brings to you, accountability, and responsibility. How you influence the world. How your internal world affects other worlds, like your children. There are all these reflection points that come with motherhood and it's made me a better person. That's not to say, if I hadn't chosen motherhood, I wouldn't be a good person, but for me, it was one of the defining moments of my life, because it gave me a different type of purpose. The responsibility of caring for another human being and the worry, the learning, and unlearning. Our parents taught us certain things. What my son and I talk about: If you're so fortunate to have a child, you get to try something different than what I did. That's the beauty of parenting. A lot of it is inherited knowledge. I raised him on St. Mark's Place, which was my dream place to live. That was my fourteen-year-old self talking. That was my forever place that I wanted to live. And my son, who was raised a city kid, as soon as he was able to make decisions for himself, he moved himself out to the suburbs, where he listens to birds chirping in the mornings and no sirens from fire trucks racing down the streets.

While raising him, I always stayed in touch with my collective mates. We've always been friends. Family. I've stayed in touch with them over the years. That's when he was at his smallest. Elementary school years, I was still active. It was a slow receding process. I would say, I can't make this show. I would prefer to do studio sessions. I didn't take tours or festivals. I missed out on some really wonderful tour experiences. I was a single mom who worked a full-time job. If I hadn't been a single mom working a full-time job, doing a month-long tour wouldn't be unheard of. To pull him out of school for a month, to hit the road for a month, wasn't possible. At the time, I worked in the business side of television. Stability was the most important thing to me in raising my son. So I slowly started backing out of those things. Over time, my collective mates understood that if I could do it and the timing was right, I would be present. If I couldn't they would do the shows without me. There was another mother in the collective, who had a similar experience. It became less and less. And what happens is, you stop writing, you stop attending events, and so you lose access to parts of your creative self. My creative practice was then mothering and my job. When I wasn't supporting those spaces, I was sleeping. I feel like things got easier when he got into high school, because he was more of an autonomous human by that time. Now he could leave the house on his own. But there were years when I did nothing, or one performance a year. As a dramatic point of comparison, since 2018, I've done over a hundred shows.

As my son is now nearing the end of his college experience, I feel like I made all the right decisions during those years. Like choosing to raise him where I did, making the sacrifices that I made. Taking him to the concerts I took him to, and exposing him to a wide variety of everything. And being able to take him on work trips around the world. One of the things I requested from my job as a single mom, was to be able to take not only him, but his godmother or another good friend, or there would be another kid with him. While I attended my work meetings in London, Berlin or other international cities, my son would have cultural experiences. That was one of the things that became important as I made the artistic sacrifices I did. Once I defined what a stable home looked like for me, I thought intentionally about what kinds of things I could inject into this situation to make it the best experience for both of us.

The mother layer does come in. The mother layer is part of the entirety of who I am at this point. I think it's everything. When I'm considering an audience, I think about how to create an experience for them that is easier to digest.

The words that I use intentionally for my recent work in the last five years, I do not curse in my work. I'd like my nieces who are five and one to be in the room where my work is being played. That was very intentional. Everyone who worked with me on this album knew that I didn't want any curses. I don't know if I'll be like that forever. This was my request for this work, and the next work. I wanted it to be played in its entirety in a room for youth, without labels or warnings on it. That was really important to me. From a music connoisseur perspective, say it how you feel it. But there have been so many times that I've walked into a space and there have been youth in the space and they're singing along to music and they don't understand the meaning. I wanted to have music that I could play for the youngest people in my life. When I was performing as a teenager, everything was coming out of our mouths. That was how we were feeling at that time. I still have an appreciation for the rawness and energy of those moments. As teenagers, I remember saying at quite a few events, I didn't realize there were going to be any children at this event. And that is the beauty of DIY spaces, where there are no age spaces. The music that's being played once you're in those spaces has the ability to do many things, good and bad. In my first album, I cover death, childhood, PTSD from growing up in a violent home. I cover things that are heavy in nature. Tough topics that many people experience, things like gun violence. I want to talk about all things, but push myself not to just curse through it. I didn't want anything I was saying to be censored. There is also the nurturing of the crowd. After the performance, being available for feedback. Before the performance, being present. The fact that I'm a mother goes into those moments. The idea that for me when someone approaches me, I am here to receive whatever that moment is offering up. I had to learn that as a parent. If my son was hurt, or just needed to have a relational moment. I just had to learn through being a mom, no matter what I'm working on, if he removed himself from wherever he was to come talk to me, I needed to do that, too. To be open to what that moment offers is the most important thing I can do. And that's how I approach the entirety of my performances. At least so far, it feels like people who attend my performances feel seen and heard. They feel connected and that's important to me, and I connect that ability and awareness to being a mother.

Music has saved my life. For me, it was the beginning of finding myself. I continue to find myself through the music. Originally, as a listener, and now as a creator. Music has been an incredible mood stabilizer, the best antidepressant I've ever experienced. It has given me my friends, and my family. I came from a family that listened to music around the clock and still needs sounds around them all the time. It's such a core part of my upbringing and relationships. It's given me so much more than I could ever give it.

Chapter 3

The Rock Mom Memoir

JULIE'S INSIGHTS

No Talking About the Baby: The Rock 'n' Roll Mom Memoir

We promote the idea that rock moms have long been rock 'n' roll heroes in their own right, aberrational women, who have shaped us like any rock star dad has (i.e., David Bowie, Keith Richards, Ozzy Osbourne). Rock mom memoirs inspire and inform our own respective under-the-radar rock mom identities—even if we're rock stars in our own minds: "A band was a magic forcefield that protected you. More than a marriage, more than family, a band said you existed, you belonged somewhere. [. . .] you'd chosen each other" (Rigby 2019, 289).

When the rock star is also a mother in the rock 'n' roll memoir, motherhood looks decidedly different. An understatement perhaps, but in the context of previous discussions here on musicking and motherhood, motherhood does not necessarily take the form of "pedagogical labor" (Savage and Hall 2017, 35), that is, "doing what's best" for the children through consciously instilling music skills and appreciation. Savage and Hall articulate the "core work" of traditionally pedagogical musicking mothers as the necessary "sacrifice of women's own desires," and that the accomplishments of one's children is how a mother defines not only her success as a mother, but her very sense of self (Savage and Hall 2021, 33). Tracing how the work of rock star moms challenge the decentering of mothers in the context of encouraging a child's musicking is just one place to enter a discussion of what we are calling the "Rock Mom Memoir," and is a compelling way to enter a chapter that will trace the myriad of ways that rock star mothers are centered and then become de-centered, "hobbled" even via the experiences of pregnancy, childbirth, and mothering, and that this is what constitutes the main dynamic and drama of the subgenre of these memoirs.

The rich qualitative interviews of chapter 2, the heart of this book, foreground the fact that our study has focused almost primarily on mothers who musick well under the radar of fame–existing on the same relative plane of participation as we do. If these under-the-radar rock moms have found fame, it has been regional, self-funded, "indie labeled," and even neighborhood based. In other words, their participation has been articulated as, in general, relatively manageable in the context of motherhood. This chapter, however, examines the trajectories and careers of rock moms, who because they have achieved quasi and outright rock stardom, struggle to manage motherhood in a high stakes profession. A quick assessment of rock memoirs, wherein the rock star also happens to be a dad, seems to reveal that the extreme challenges of doing both does not exist for male rockers, or if it does, the experience is not significant enough to write about, or is contextualized by a father's absence and/or aberrational "bad boy" behavior. For example, in '80s hair metal band founder Sebastian Bach's rock memoir, *18 and Life on Skid Row,* Bach alludes to his infant son with guilt, because he's cheating on the son's mother while on tour (Bach 2016, 146). In reading published rock mom memoirs–and again these books are not marketed as such–motherhood intrudes. The difficulties inherent of "doing both" takes up a lot more space. For this reason, an analysis of rock mom memoirs as primary source material provides an important context against which the original qualitative data gathered from the rock women we know might be compared.

This look at famous mothers in rock exists in the context of the many rock women who chose not to have children. These women see motherhood and rock 'n' roll as a binary that cannot be conflated. One must choose one or the other. In a 2002 article with *InStyle* magazine, Fleetwood Mac member and solo artist Stevie Nicks starkly underscores this "' . . . Do you want to be an artist and a writer, or a wife and a lover? With kids, your focus changes. I don't want to go to PTA meetings'" (Finn 2014, para. 2). From our interview with the parents of Ruyter Seys, guitar player and founding member of the Atlanta-founded hard rock band Nashville Pussy, we learned that their daughter decided that a commitment to her career and the demands of frequent touring made having a child impossible. The rock mom memoirs gathered for this chapter shows that with few exceptions, rock star mom life exerts demands beyond the conventionally articulated challenges of the non-rock working mother. At the very least, a few mothers of our memoir sample report that even famous rock moms have the same challenges as any working mom. Sonic Youth bassist and founding member Kim Gordon writes in her memoir about being frustrated by interviewers' questions regarding what it's like to be a working mother in rock: "It's a question I could never answer to my, nor anyone else's satisfaction without giving one of those 'Like any woman balancing a family and a job' answer–the most boring one I could think of" (2015, 221).

Gordon's resigned admission cuts into popular conceptions of rock 'n' roll fame. Referencing Sebastian Bach's rock memoir, the demands and attractions of a heavy music lifestyle is always articulated as an adolescent romance characterized by sex, drugs, speed, freedom—an ideal that is "unfettered and alive," to quote Joni Mitchell in her track "Free Man in Paris," written in the persona of rock mogul David Geffen (Mitchell 1974). As well, rock draws its allure and power from the fantasy that the rock 'n' roll lifestyle and its loci are risky even for grown-ups. In other words, children, whose central mission is to fetter their parents and be a general drag on adult fun, undermine this fantasy. As Pat Benatar's record company, Chrysalis admonished her, after the birth of her first daughter in 1985: "'No one wants to see a rocker who's someone's mother. Mothers aren't sexy" (Benatar 2010, 163).

Given the unconventional workspaces of performing rock musicians, the demands placed on them by everyone from record companies, to band members to fans, rock mom memoirs reveal, despite Gordon's pat response to interviewers, that the balancing of rock mom life is considerably more precarious than that of non-rock working moms. Any account of a woman's participation in rock 'n' roll is a story of barriers constructed by an extremely sexist music industry, run almost exclusively by men, within a male-dominated culture. This structural sexism that Benatar notes in her memoir was more of a factor when she was breaking into the business in the '70s and '80s (2010, 239) is exacerbated by additional challenges that women rockers face when they become mothers. In doing so, we foreground–perhaps for the first time—that the rock 'n' roll mom memoir is a subgenre into itself, and one that should be studied apart from the mass of published rock 'n' roll memoirs. Indeed, since the '90s, the number of book-length memoirs, authored by rock stars and published by major publishing houses, has grown exponentially in both quantity and quality. Notable examples are Rolling Stones guitarist Keith Richards, whose memoir *Life*, reached number four on *The New York Times* nonfiction best-seller list in 2010. In the same year, rock mom Patti Smith's memoir *Just Kids* won a National Book Award. Quipped a book editor to *The New York Times* in 2011, "It appears that the entire Rock and Roll Hall of Fame is now sitting in front of the computer" (Bosman 2011). By the '90s and in ensuing decades, performers at the height of their fame in the '80s and '90s have, over the past decades, reached the natural age to write a memoir, and this happens to include rock 'n' roll mothers.

We want to make the case here that the rock mom memoir, because of the complex exigencies of mothering in an inhospitable context, is the most compelling of the rock memoir genre in a sea of stories about rock 'n' roll men.

In music writer Rob Sheffield's 2020 *Rolling Stone* article "The 50 Greatest Rock Memoirs of All Time," only ten of the fifty memoirs compiled were written by female-identified rockers, and of these ten, only five chronicle the lives of rock mothers, whose narratives, it goes without saying, include elements unique to this subgenre. It is the incongruity of the events and challenges within a rock context that make the rock mom narrative uncommon and compelling.

The conventional rock 'n' roll memoir often opens with the rocker at his lowest point in various iterations of distress, riddled with addiction, dropped by his label, being sued for alimony and child support by exes and financially strapped. The narrative then cycles back to childhood, chronicling the arduous and fortuitous rise to fame, with disruptions of addiction battles, marriage and lovers, medical issues, bad managers, and of course, the cynical, whimsical, and mendacious music industry. All of these are potential disruptors along the path of rock stardom—and life in general. In stark contrast to the rock mom memoir, none of the male rockers' careers shape themselves around the imperatives of pregnancy, childbirth, and parenting. Record labels aren't annoyed that a pregnancy will upend a male rocker's monetized sex appeal. And while many of male rock memoir authors are dads—Sebastian Bach, Peter Criss, Duff McKagan, to name a few—assiduous details of their respective partners' pregnancies and birth, touring with children, sexism from record companies and management are largely missing from their respective published memoirs.

In contrast, the rock mom story is rife with details about pregnancy, fertility, abortions, more pregnancy, subsequent record company pushback, birth, and mothering—all which must be managed while fulfilling the obligations of a touring and recording musician in one of the most demanding professions. The rock mom narrative, an extreme version of the working mom narrative, is a landscape of often startling and stark juxtaposition. The rock mom memoir may be the only written context conflating the complex labor of mothering with the high demand labor of rocking, which is often where the narrative conflict resides. In her 2010 memoir, *Between a Heart and a Rock Place*, Pat Benatar reports being left to navigate this complex situation on her own: "I knew women who were married to rock stars and who had their babies with them when they traveled. But when I had Haley, I knew few female rock stars to begin with, let alone female rock stars with babies. There's no handbook for being a rocker girl with a newborn baby" (160). Perhaps this chapter, in surveying the narratives of rock moms who "made it," can function as a handbook.

Defining the Sample

While a variety of rock mom memoirs will be referred to, this chapter focuses on nine rock mom memoirs, in particular. In gathering the sample, consideration was made to include those where the advent of mothering disrupts established music careers. For this reason, founding Pretenders member Chrissie Hynde's 2015 memoir *Reckless* was not included, as she ends her story just as the Pretenders ascend, and before Hynde becomes a mother. The Go-Go's bassist Kathy Valentine's 2020 memoir, *All I Ever Wanted*, which tracks her life and career before the birth of her daughter, and includes a poignant section on her pre-Roe abortion at the age of twelve—a crucial element of any mothering narrative—was not included. Likewise, Los Angeles punk rocker Alice Bag's memoir *Violence Girl* was excluded, as motherhood appears as only as a brief mention: the phrase "I had a baby" is near the end of two-page epilogue (2011, 380). Patti Smith's *Just Kids*, her acclaimed self-portrait of the artist as a young woman, brings in the baby only at memoir's end: "Robert [Mapplethorpe] was diagnosed with AIDS at the same time I found I was carrying my second child" (2010, 265), during which she was already on hiatus from the music career she built in the '70s. Drummer Patty Schemel doesn't introduce her daughter into her rock mom story until the penultimate chapter of her 2017 memoir *Hit So Hard*. When Schemel becomes a mother with her wife, she's already lost her drummer spot in the '90s band Hole due to severe drug abuse. Hence, this short section on motherhood is a point of redemption and healing in her harrowing story. Schemel writes that "Becoming a parent is like getting married and then opening up a small business together. It's a lot of charts, meetings, and negotiations, it's a 24-hour-a-day job" (255). For Schemel, as with our other rock moms, rock does not stop with motherhood: Schemel's daughter "refers to any band I'm in as 'Mom's Rock 'n' Roll,' and she asks for it by name: 'Let's play Mom's Rock 'n' Roll'" (2017, 257).

The mothers featured here have given other women a roadmap for their own rock lives to come. Established and appropriate contexts for women in music are split open by rock women of the '60s and '70s, and provide moments of giddiness in these memoirs. While watching Suzi Quatro perform on television for the first time, future Go-Go's bassist Kathy Valentine writes that Quatro was so different from women musicians who "held acoustic guitars or sat at pianos." For Valentine, experiencing Suzi Quatro is a paradigm shifting experience "that had the same effect as lightning bolts shooting through my grandma's house, with thunder blasting along. Where do I go, what do I do, who am I?" (2020, 51–52).

A few years older than Valentine, teenaged Viv Albertine was also looking implicitly to be inspired by rock women. In staid and sexist '70s-era England, she "studied the record covers for the names of girlfriends and wives. [. . .]

scanned the thank-yous and the lyrics looking for girls' names" (2015, 49). Picking up future fellow rock mom Patti Smith's debut album *Horses* while a student in art school in 1975, Albertine writes that the album gave her permission to "risk falling flat on her face" (2015, 79–80). Patti Smith, who eventually would break from music to become a wife and mother in the '80s, also gives Albertine permission to actively musick in rock: "Every cell of my body was steeped in music," Albertine asserts, "but it never occurred to me that I could be in a band, not in a million years–why would I? Who'd done it before me? There was no one I could identify with. No girls played electric guitar. Especially not ordinary girls like me" (2015, 49).

While other chapters here examine the experiences of non-musician mothers who musick in rock culture, the rock memoirs gathered for this one feature musician mothers only, with the assumption that non-musician musicking mothers are not bound by the extreme imperatives of music careers: record label obligations, including multi-city tours and maintaining album contracts. Although Jessica Hopper's interview in chapter 2 challenges this assertion, in order to limit the sample, we started from the assumption that non-musician musicking mothers can pull away to mother, or more easily integrate rock musicking and mothering. For this reason, the memoirs of non-musician musicking mothers were excluded, among them famous rock groupie Pamela Des Barres's memoir of marriage and motherhood, *Take Another Little Piece of My Heart: A Groupie Grows Up*, her 1993 follow up to her iconic 1987 memoir, *I'm with the Band: Confessions of a Rock Groupie*. Likewise, hair metal video model and rock wife Bobbie Brown's 2013 memoir *Dirty Rocker Boys* was also not considered for this study. Also, and perhaps surprisingly excluded from the sample was Kristin Hersh's powerful 2020 memoir *Seeing Sideways: A Memoir of Music and Motherhood*, which solely exists to chronicle a touring mother/musician's life with four children in a van. Hersh's story is powerful and necessary, but the focus of our sample is on published memoirs where the biological and logistical imperatives, the necessary labor of mothering complicate, disrupt, even upend established music careers. In other words, the attempt was to include memoirs not explicitly marketed as stories about mothers. Motherhood is the surprise Easter egg in what became the final sample.

The list for this study was narrowed to nine published memoirs. They are as follows:

Viv Albertine, 2014, *Clothes, Clothes, Clothes. Music, Music, Music. Boys, Boys, Boys*
Pat Benatar, 2010, *Between a Heart and a Rock Place*
Belinda Carlisle, 2010, *Lips Unsealed*
Lita Ford, 2016, *Living like a Runaway*

Kim Gordon, 2015, *Girl in a Band*
Grace Jones, 2015, *I'll Never Write My Memoirs*
Suzy Quatro, 2008, *UnZipped*
Amy Rigby, 2019, *Girl to City*
Tina Turner, 2018, *My Love Story*

In terms of demographics, eight of the nine authors are baby boomers, born between 1946 and 1964. Only one of the nine, Tina Turner, born in 1939, is from the silent generation. In spite of the fact that rock 'n' roll was essentially invented by Black women, only two of the mothers in the list are Black. Aesthetic boundaries can be porous and interrogated, but in general, throughout this book, attention has been paid to mothers who musick in relatively "hard music" genres. While Grace Jones might be thought of as a disco or dance music artist, it's impossible not to consider a song like "Demolition Man" as emerging from a distinct "hard music" space, both musically, lyrically, and in Jones's aggressive performance in the accompanying music video. This book list's range also accounts for a variety of music success stories, including rock icons with an enormous reach like world famous actor/model/musician Jones and Grammy winner and two-time Rock and Roll Hall of Fame inductee Tina Turner, who is commonly referred to as the "queen of rock 'n' roll" (Benetiz-Eves, 2022). This list also includes "indie" artists like Amy Rigby and post-punk mom Viv Albertine, the latter of whom disappeared from music for twenty-five years after the demise of

Figure 3.1. Grace Jones in music video for "Demolition Man."
Source: Screenshot

her groundbreaking all-female band, The Slits. In other words, a rock mom does not have to have achieved peak success in the music business–millions of album sales, sold out stadiums, and music awards–to have been considered impactful enough to publish and sell a rock memoir. Indeed, influential rock mom and acclaimed Sonic Youth bass player Kim Gordon, whose book *Girl in a Band* made our list, refers to herself as "barely famous" (Tipton 2019).

All of these memoirs' authors, however, would have been in either early adulthood or early mid-adulthood and affected to some degree by the rise of second-wave white feminism in the '60s, at least partially incited by Betty Friedan's best-selling 1963 book, *The Feminine Mystique*. Second-wave feminists were crucial voices in a culture that disenfranchised women at every turn. When rock moms Cher and Tina Turner were beginning careers, women weren't allowed to have their own bank accounts. Tina references the cruel irony part and parcel of employed women in her memoir *My Love Story*: "Many women in the '60s and '70s relied on their husbands to take care of the business of life, but [Cher and I] were in the funny position of making all the money without having any control over our income" (2018, 104). Friedan's *The Feminine Mystique* addressed this structural inequity. The result of a survey of white middle-class suburban women who reported their frustrations with their limited roles as wife and mothers, *The Feminine Mystique* was less about an outright rejection of men and motherhood, which was Friedan's complaint of many second-wave feminists. In it, Friedan proposed a radical reconfiguration of structures and dynamics that required mothers assume the majority of child rearing and homemaking, which Friedan frames as historically limiting structures that narrowed their life choices (Zeitz 2008, 687). This rejection of traditional women's roles is not necessarily consciously referred to in the titles examined by this chapter, all but nine of the rock moms chose a life as professional rock musicians independently before choosing marriage/partnering and motherhood. Seven of the nine rock moms of these respective titles met their partners/fathers of their child[ren] through music participation. Roughly half found their husbands/fathers of their children in their respective bands. All but one of the mothers in the sample met their partners/father of their child(ren) through the entertainment industry.

Referencing Friedan and second-wave feminism here should signify that this discussion is a relatively historical and decidedly conventional. For example, all of the mothers in this sample are straight and cis-gendered, and identity as female. At least partially due to the fact that memoirs are written when there has been a sufficient amount of life lived, all of our sample's authors are in late middle age or seniors, coming into consciousness decades before discussions of LGBTQIA issues or gender non-binary were mainstream, in wide circulation. To the best of our knowledge, there is not yet a published rock mom memoir whose author is defined from a historically marginalized gendered or sexual identity. We are confident that someday there will be.

As aforementioned, none of the books in the sample have been marketed as rock mom memoirs. These books are not the rock version of Anne Lamott's best-selling mothering memoir *Operating Instructions: A Journal of My Son's First Year*, but at the same time, this study examines memoirs that feature women dealing with the shock of caring for an infant. They do so in a context where the author is the public face, influence, signature of a well-known band, a key creator, if not its founder. Essentially, these are rock 'n' roll stories first in which a competing and compelling mothering narrative unfolds. Amy Rigby, contextualizes her rock story to come, implicitly alluding to popular '80s texts like the "yuppie" film *Baby Boom* in her memoir *Girl to City*, about coming to Manhattan for art school in the '70s and making a life there: "The concept of women who did it all, career and motherhood, had grown steadily throughout the eighties. But I only knew two mothers, and they were the opposite of businesswomen" (Rigby 2019, 218).

The sexism of the music industry is prominent in the face of these artists' respective pregnancies. Chrysalis record executives, irked that Benatar married her guitarist Neil Giraldo, have an extreme reaction after she gets pregnant while making the band's fifth studio album, *Tropico* (2010, 153–54). (In fact, she experiences morning sickness during the shooting of the video for "We Belong" off the album [2010, 157].) In her memoir, Benatar writes about pushing back against Chrysalis, as she would have to do continuously: "Being pregnant permeated the entire [creative] process. Pregnancy makes all the long muscles in the body relax, and your vocal cords are a long muscle" (2010, 156). Despite Benatar asserting that pregnancy makes her a better, even more acrobatic singer, Chrysalis wanted her pregnancy to be a guarded secret. "This was the '80s," Benatar writes, "and I was a married woman, yet Chrysalis treated me like some Hollywood starlet from the fifties who'd been knocked up out of wedlock" (2010, 157). Benatar points out that although Chrysalis "had spent years objectifying [her]," they wanted no photos of Benatar once she started to show, and no talking about babies during interviews (2010, 157–58). "My pregnancy was something to be ashamed of instead of celebrated" [. . .] (2010, 158).

This discussion will align itself along a decidedly obvious progression through what might be a standard chronological mothering narrative: pregnancy, birth, motherhood/mothering. While the moment mothering starts might be another disputed boundary, this one, political, the mothering portion of this chronology begins after birth. Of the mothers here, Tina Turner is the only teenage mother, with her first pregnancy coming at the age of eighteen, the father being not future husband Ike Turner, but Ike's touring band's saxophonist. This unplanned young adult pregnancy is juxtaposed with Benatar's above, who had given up getting pregnant (2018, 155), and the respective fertility journeys of Suzy Quatro, age thirty-two when pregnant with her first child, and Viv Albertine's harrowing IVF journey and resultant pregnancy at age forty-four, when after a C-section, she discovers she has a tumor on her cervix, which begins a cancer battle as she's caring for her newborn. Former Runaways guitarist and heavy metal solo artist, Lita Ford became pregnant after many attempts at age thirty-eight. The Go-Go's Belinda Carlisle, however, was ambivalent about getting pregnant and regarded the prospect negatively: "Part of me was horrified" [. . .] "I feared that my life as I knew it . . . was about to end" (2010, 162). In the memoir, Carlisle is as unfiltered about her pregnancy complications as she is about her drug abuse, admitting that before learning she was pregnant, she had "binged on coke and done ecstasy" (2010, 164), and that adverse pregnancy symptoms were conflated with the demands of her rock career: "I had a rough bout of morning sickness that went all the way through my promotional tour of Europe and Scandinavia" (167), and that because of a diagnosis of "severe toxemia" (167), she . . . "looked distorted and gross" (167) and was put on bedrest.

While Grace Jones reveals the complexities of a rock 'n' roll pregnancy in her memoir, revealing that the first thing she does after finding out she is pregnant is give up quaaludes, she manages to fold in celebrity glamor: Andy Warhol and Blondie's Debbie Harry throw her a star-studded baby shower at downtown Manhattan gay disco, the Garage (207). Jones initially feels none of Carlisle's ambivalence: she "instinctively felt [pregnancy] would be a powerful, positive thing." She "hardly showed, at seven months pregnant, and had no morning sickness, none of the classic symptoms of pregnancy." Jones writes at first about feeling "normal" with "a lot of energy," but then reports a more complex experience: "the baby started to move inside of me, and that was very alien. [. . .] Now and then I would panic, wondering how it was going to come out of that hole" (Jones 2015, 216). Jones's pregnancy, like Carlisle's, ends in medically mandated bedrest. But while Carlisle's is due to a medical issue, Jones's suddenly complex pregnancy, according to her assessment, is incited by a dramatic break-in and hold-up in her Manhattan apartment, during which she convinces the gunman to untie her. Writes Jones, "The hold-up had accelerated the pregnancy and I was close to being due weeks before the baby had fully developed. I had to spend weeks resting" (2015, 219).

In her memoir, heavy metal mom Lita Ford writes about doggedly pursuing a solo career when she decides to marry the future father of her two sons. This is ironically where the memoir becomes bleak (2016, 200). In 1995, she released her solo album *Black* in response to the rise of grunge music. When Ford becomes pregnant, she's in a period where as an artist she feels "beaten down, exhausted." Writing from hindsight, Ford constructs an ominous tone:

Quitting music for fourteen years to "be the loyal and faithful wife" [. . .] "would be the most disastrous decision of my life." Referencing her album title, *Black*, Lita writes, "The next decade and a half of my life would be a nightmare, a silent scream. I withdrew from the music industry and faded to black" (2016, 202). Pregnancy eludes her awhile, and referencing the handbook metaphor Benatar uses in her memoir, the idea of being a parent confounds her: "Kids don't come with a manual, they don't have six strings. You can't hit pause or mute, and there's no standby switch" (2016, 208). "I read a lot of books on pregnancy and how to be a great mother. I set a high bar for myself: I wanted to be just like my mom [. . .] for the first time since I left music, I had a focus" (2016, 209).

Sonic Youth bassist Kim Gordon writes in her memoir *Girl in a Band* that in her mid-thirties she "started looking at babies," but "could never figure out the best time to start a family. . . . " It was her husband and bandmate Thurston Moore who convinced [her] that "we could carry the parenting thing off" (2015, 219). As with other rock moms of our sample, pregnancy and performing is conflated: "Four-months pregnant. I managed to wriggle into a miniskirt for our 'Bull in the Heather' video" (2015, 194). She is similarly open about the challenges of taking care of oneself while pregnant and being in a band, and even more so when one has two bands: "When I started Free Kitten [. . .] I remember having an amnio and taking the rest of the day off. When I was eight-and-a-half months pregnant, Sonic Youth appeared on *Late Night with David Letterman*. The machine never stopped, even though what I really wanted to do was lie down, all the time, in part because I had a fibroid tumor that grew with the baby" (2015, 197–98). Gordon not only reports feeling overwhelmed and exhausted during pregnancy, but also anxious about becoming a mother: "Being pregnant made me nervous. In my third trimester, I remember going to a party where I ran into Peter Buck of REM. I was frightened to hold their baby. I also had a series of anxiety dreams" (2015, 220).

Indie rocker Amy Rigby assiduously details rock life while pregnant in her memoir *Girl to City*. Experiencing pregnancy during a low budget rock tour is cast as wholly unpleasant and Rigby reports having no model for this. Perhaps the most under-the-radar rock mom of all of those in the sample, Rigby provides perhaps the most complete picture of rock 'n' rolling while pregnant. Underscoring our assertion that rock mom memoirs are easily the most compelling ones, Rigby's details of touring while pregnant are when her narrative is at its most unfiltered and raw: "five months pregnant" I "woke up sweating on a pile of equipment in the back of a van" (2019, 206), "queasy with morning sickness." [. . .] In New Orleans, "Eating crawfish filled [her] with revulsion" (2019, 207). Rigby's memoir stands out in that in it we see a rock mom assert that she should be treated with greater care than the non-pregnant members of her band: "All I asked for was hourly meals, a bed to sleep in, and the lone passenger seat in the van." Still, Rigby insists on loading and unloading the van in hopes that "regular exercise" will make the birth easier (2019, 213). A major takeaway from the "pregnancy" sections in Rigby's memoir are the ones that assert a conflation of the two identities. Like many of these rock moms, music had been a motivating force in Rigby's life and crucial to identity formation. She simply can't fathom choosing between rocking and mothering and that she will make all best efforts to do both: "post-tour . . . I'd briefly fantasized that becoming a mother would put a definitive stop to musical pipe dreams. [. . .] I hadn't factored in how music [. . .] was such a part of my identity, I didn't know who I'd be if I stopped. [. . .] If I stayed home with this baby [. . .] wouldn't I be like my mother, dependent on a man for money and on my children to live out my dreams?" (2019, 208).

This book took its working title from the intense visceral experience of pregnancy. The subjects of our qualitative interviews conflated loud music with the movement of fetuses in utero. Rigby textualizes pregnancy and musicking as follows: "I ate bbq in every state, avoided alcohol and cigarettes and onstage I felt the baby kick, especially when I thumped the upsight bass and struggled with the accordion" (2019, 214). This conflation extends to descriptions of rock 'n' roll maternity wear. Unlike passages in Turner's and Benatar's respective narratives wherein a pregnancy had to be hidden for a career, Rigby flaunts hers: "As opposed to the 'big smocks with bows' my mother had worn. I still wanted to dress like myself. Spandex was popular and Amanda made stretchy black skirts and leggings with red and black stripes up the side and orange and red flames down the other" (2019, 218). On stage at CBGB, "Now I was treading those wormy boards seven months pregnant and one day my future baby could say that she/he had played there too." At CBGB, Rigby flaunts a "short dress over [a] growing belly," as well as revising the classic rock 'n' roll sexual stance, first popularized by Elvis, of a guitar over a pelvis: "My acoustic guitar sat out away from my hips, and I strummed with a new authority" (2019, 220). A front-facing pregnant identity dramatically revises the rock 'n' roll stage gestalt: the pregnant rock stance separates the guitar from the pelvis, where it had conventionally lived.

Like Rigby, Quatro wants her pregnancy to be visually prominent so that the public will know she's "normal" as opposed to a rock mom aberration: "I didn't show early which pissed me off." Yet like Rigby, Quatro also wants to eschew the classic "maternity look" of the times: "I never bought any maternity clothes but just wore my usual jeans with an extension sewn in and one of Len's Levi shirts. Even though I was pregnant I was desperate to hang on to the image of Suzi Quatro. Somewhere inside I was afraid this child would change everything and of course it did" (234). As aforementioned, Benatar's record company wouldn't allow her pregnancy to be visually prominent, insisting that no one get a photo of her while pregnant. Benatar begrudgingly bowed to the pressure that '80s-era record companies could assert by wearing "big coats and loose clothing to hide it" (2010, 158). Tina Turner's passages of being pregnant on stage in the late '50s into 1960 foreground how difficult it was in that era to conflate visual iterations of motherhood with rock 'n' roll. As opposed to Rigby's, Turner's stagewear was designed to obscure impending motherhood. In her memoir, Turner describes how pregnancy does not impede her frenzied performance: "Ike was uneasy during the [Apollo Theater] show because I was moving around so much and I was in an advanced state of pregnancy. He tried to rein me in [. . .] but I twisted and did the Pony right up until I gave birth in October. My dresses were designed to hide the baby, which was not easy to do because I was carrying a boy and my belly was pointed. . . . I wore a tight, straight underdress that held everything in, with a loose chiffon layer on top to camouflage the 'bump.' I was so young that I had boundless energy and stamina. I felt wonderful the whole time I was pregnant" (2018, 50–51).

In the third trimester of pregnancy. Turner ups the ante for legions of punk performers to come, when she "jumps into the pit at the Apollo." Writes Turner, "I didn't look like I was in my eighth month, which was a good thing. I think people would have been really nervous about that! But the baby was never in danger. Honestly, it wasn't that big a drop and I was a good athlete. I knew that I could handle it" (2018, 51). Quatro, however, writes that pregnancy and birth would disrupt her rock moves, "even though we had work booked, it would just have to be postponed—you can't jump around on stage with a baby growing inside" (242).

Being pregnant can hinder not just stage moves, but also a rock mom's relationship to creativity. A pregnant Rigby notes that "The songs weren't coming as quickly as they had before, if at all" (2019, 218). At the time, Rigby was married to touring musician Will Rigby, drummer for the dBs. Performing while pregnant, Rigby asks herself a question that her husband probably does not: "Out on the road, I asked myself how much longer I could be in a band. In five months, I was going to have a baby to take care of. How was it possible to do both? The answer had already been decided for me. I'd started another band" (2019, 214).

In her memoir *Unzipped*, legendary bassist of the band she fronted and television sitcom Happy Days' Leather Tuscadero, Suzi Quatro writes that the journey to become pregnant was as difficult as her journey to have a viable career in music. Her pregnancy comes after forming a band under the tutelage of English producer Mickey Most and a marriage to her band's guitarist, Len Tuckey. In her memoir, she writes of "low fertility and a tilted womb," blaming the rock "lifestyle" (225), and secretly fears she will never have children (226). After a cycle of fertility drugs, she becomes pregnant (225), and presents at the British rock awards in her first trimester (227). Famous for being a small woman who powerfully wields a low-slung bass guitar on stage, pregnancy takes her out: at one point she's "in bed in a hotel room feeling sick. Tired." and almost "[falls] asleep waiting to go onstage with Dire Straits" (228). Quatro is devastated by the resultant miscarriage and sees that as undercutting any professional progress she has made in her life: "I had failed. I could tour the world and entertain, but produce a healthy baby? Oh, no. As a woman, I felt like a no-hoper." Quatro writes with painful honesty about the trauma of miscarrying: "I felt like such a pathetic idiot . . . the emotional recovery would take months and months. I drank too much. I cried all the time" (230). "I was down, down, down. . . . Gigs were quickly arranged, as Len thought this would be the best therapy. . . . Had I done too much work? Should I have flown to Australia, especially at that risky early stage before a pregnancy really takes hold? Basically, I blamed myself" (233). For Quatro, overcoming her grief is possible, not by playing more gigs, but by getting pregnant again, which she does, without fertility drugs.

In addition to her grief, Quatro must endure abuse from her husband, Len Tuckey. He joins Ike Turner in our discussion, as a rock 'n' roll husband, who inflicts trauma upon the rock mom, the visual and emotional center of their respective bands. In providing Tuckey's messaging to her, Quatro underscores the extreme pressure she's under as a center of the band who also provides the family with children: "I suppose you think you're fucking clever, don't you? There's a Suzi Quatro album due out in April—so how the fuck are we supposed to promote it with a baby in your belly?" (233). Despite this, Quatro's high risk pregnancy took precedence over touring: "Obviously, I couldn't tour and was ordered to take it easy. So I began nine months of home life in such an unnatural way for me to live and soon grew bored." Still, she is emotionally juggling, trying to take care of herself and appease her husband/bandmate at the same time, "I promised Len we would go back on the road and earn our living as soon as the baby came. I insisted from day one that whatever children we were lucky to have would travel with us and not be left at home. This might lose us some work, but I didn't care. I was adamant." (234). In this era, when second-wave feminism was still new, the culture was still seeing women's roles in terms of opposing dichotomies: "My unexpected pregnancy had caused us to delay our Australian tour. I looked absolutely exhausted. Most of the interviews centered on the dichotomy of Suzi Quatro and Mum living in the same skin. How was this possible?" (247).

For Turner, like Quatro heading up the machine of her band, there is almost no space as a rock 'n' roll mom for resolving the two imperatives, and Turner feels a similar pressure to keep the rock machine going: "Our crazy touring routine left no time for family life. I almost gave birth to our son, Robie, while we were still on that first tour. Ike noticed I was about to deliver and rerouted us to a hospital in Los Angeles, where we were booked at some clubs. He expected me to have the baby and bounce right back. Two days after becoming a mother, I was onstage, singing and dancing as if nothing had happened. The reality was, if I didn't sing, there was no show, and no show meant no money" (Turner 2018, 55).

Carlisle's birth narrative is troubled not only by pregnancy complications, but also by elements of conventional rock narratives that involve drugs. Her son, Duke is three weeks early, and the lack of amniotic fluid means Carlisle has an "emergency C-section" (167). Her baby in the neo-natal intensive care unit (NICU), she goes back and forth to bring him pumped milk (169). Carlisle writes of the added stress of being grilled by the doctor regarding cocaine use during pregnancy (171). Carlisle's ambivalence and "prolonged state of shock and denial about being a mother as well as an addict" is palpable: "I was loving and nurturing . . . I wasn't available as I should have been. I could have done better" (170).

Heavy metal mom Lita Ford, anticipates motherhood, in spite of her high-risk pregnancy, and ends her passage on this experience redemptively with an allusion to her life in rock 'n' roll: "I read a lot of books on pregnancy and how to be a great mother. I set a high bar for myself: I wanted to be just like my mom [. . .] for the first time since I left music, I had a focus." But like Albertine and Carlisle in their respective memoirs, Ford is open about the trauma–the "bleeding and bedrest" (209)—so often part and parcel of the maternity journey. The birth of her first son in 1997 ends in a C-section: "I started bleeding badly, and I got really scared. I sat on a black towel humiliated because I was with a stranger." Ford labors for twelve hours without dilating, and worries that she might lose the baby. After being "cut open," the "weight of the baby" recedes, and the trauma is mixed with joy: "Suddenly I could breathe, which I hadn't been able to do for months prior. James was screaming. [. . .] He was so fucking loud that I thought, Oh, God, another lead singer! I fell in love instantly" (210). Rigby also makes a rock 'n' roll allusion upon the first time seeing her daughter: "Hazel was immediately her own person, with huge eyes that stared out knowingly and a mod hairdo straight out of the Small Faces" (224).

Grace Jones, as well, concludes her birth story in the unconventional context of a music career. While these famous moms present us birth stories in the conventionally unfiltered fashion of them, Jones's is presented in a crisp elliptical fashion: "Feeling pressure. Sat on the toilet and began to push. I had no labor pains. I pushed and pushed. It turns out it was the baby. Another half an hour and I would have given birth in the bathroom at home. I was feeling pressure, no pain" (219). [. . .] "Within a half hour Paulo was born" (220). Conflating music and motherhood, Jones writes that her celebrity photographer husband Jean Paul Goude, in the delivery room the whole time, takes the opportunity to turn a moment of Jones's labor into resonant album cover art: "Years later, he would use my expression as I gave my final push before our son appeared, my mouth stretched as wide as it could for the cover of *Slave to the Rhythm*, one of his most amazing images—he extended the last big scream, the birth moment, made my mouth impossibly open" (220).

Quatro contributes another astonishing image when writing about trying to receive an epidural during labor. The labor and logistics involved in her performance negatively affects her maternal labor. Her rock work has made administering an epidural during labor a problem: "after years of carrying a heavy bass around on my back, there was no space. [My spine's] like one long bone" (2008, 245).

While Jones writes of the fact that though her husband "saw everything" in the delivery room, he still wanted to have sex with her (2015, 220), Quatro writes about the distress that birth and motherhood has on her bandmate husband: "Len's not a hands-on dad. He left everything to me. . . . I guess lots of men are like that, but it pissed me off. I was bringing in the money, being, if you like, the mum *and* the dad. Another nail in the coffin of my marriage. For the first time, I started to feel used. Sexually we were off track, too. You just can't see a C-section and fall back into bed. After trying so hard to have our baby, I wanted more" (2008, 240).

The Go-Go's Carlisle takes a break until her son Duke is one, and dovetails her new mothering experience with the conventional demands of working mothers–albeit those who have nannies: "It was a juggling act familiar to other mothers. My days were full. I played with Duke, helped organize his day with the nanny, planned most meals" home "was filled with the toys and chaos of busy lives" (173). Gordon corroborates the depiction of motherhood as a "juggling act." Despite taking time off after her daughter Coco's birth, there were always things happening: "artists are never truly on vacation." Sonic Youth is still touring and Gordon, "still breastfeeding," jetlagged and has a baby "who didn't sleep through the night" (2015, 198). Benatar underscores this experience: "Haley wasn't even sleeping through the night. I was up and down at all hours breastfeeding her and living in a state of perpetual exhaustion. I was in no position to do anything, let alone write, rehearse, and record an album" (2010, 165).

Giving birth in the '90s—in an era after Quatro, and some of the other mothers here—Gordon writes of the parenting inequities that persist along gendered lines no matter what the decade. Despite the general liberation of being accepted as a "girl in a band," the inequitable structures of parenting—"in what they'd hoped would be an equal division of labor"—only highlight a feeling of alienation: "Like most new moms, I found that no matter how just and shared you expect the experience to be, or how equal the man thinks parenting should be, it isn't. It can't be. Most child-raising falls on women's shoulders." Gordon contributes to the accruing instances of the physicality of motherhood throughout the memoirs: " . . . whenever Coco cried I felt it immediately, physically, because my breasts began to leak. Thurston [. . .] would never feel that same kind of urgency, that desire to make the crying stop" (2015, 220). A bit later in the narrative, Gordon complains that she alone is the parent "thinking ahead to scheduling a sitter for tours. Thurston didn't have the same kind of forethought" (243). Rigby's experience of the differences between rock moms and rock dads underscores Gordon's words: "When Will was away, I felt like a single parent, trying to find places for Hazel to spend the night when I had a show or a rehearsal. When Will was home and I went away, I still felt responsible for taking care of Hazel" (2019, 263).

Gordon's alienation as a new mother is compounded by the move from New York City to Massachusetts, so that Coco can experience a more conventional life (2015, 234), but in the country "No other parents came from a rock and roll world. No one else was going on tour and coming home to figure out what's next" (2015, 231). Although two of four members of Sonic Youth are not Coco's parents, the entire band bends around her. The following passage details how band travel now includes the child's needs and items, that unlike band equipment, are non-essentials for rock 'n' roll: "Until she was about ten, Coco always came with us. [. . .] Touring with a child was nerve wracking. Packing, unpacking, rushing to get planes, boarding a van to the hotel and then to sound check. In airports, Beanie Babies call out every fifty feet. Disciplining a child in public is no picnic" (2015, 232). Benatar also writes of the logistical complications of taking a child on a rock tour sans nanny. And like Gordon, Benatar is also married to her band's guitarist: "In our case, we had the same schedule. If I was working, Spyder was working. It was a logistical challenge. We didn't want to hire a nanny to take care of this baby we'd waited so long to have. [. . .] It's the same struggle all working parents go through. I wanted to stay home, but I knew it would be a mistake professionally and Chrysalis did not waste an opportunity to remind me of that" (2010, 165). Both Benatar and Quatro write about the grind of having a child on the road, even if a nanny is present. In the case of Quatro about to embark on a sold-out tour, this time as a mother: "There I was back in the jumpsuit again, but it was quite an adjustment touring with a baby. Usually my off time on tour was spent resting my voice and lazing around until gig time. Those days were gone, but it sure got me back in shape again. [My daughter] was soon a road veteran" (2008, 239). Benatar is far less sanguine about the adjustment. During an interview about how she prepares for a show, she tells an interviewer: "I'm standing in the bus trying to put on mascara for the show. My two-year-old is sitting on the potty saying, 'Mommy, wipe me!' That's how I get ready" (2010, 161).

In addition to managing the physical and logistical aspects of having a baby, Gordon writes that she is expected to respond to interviewers' questions regarding how she manages her gender and identity: "Having a baby created a huge identity crisis inside of me. It didn't help that during press interviews, journalists always said 'What's it like to be a rock-and-roll mom?' just as over the last decades they couldn't help asking, 'What's it like to be a girl in a band?'" (2015, 221). Perhaps Quatro answered the question asked of Gordon, again personal questions from interviewers that husbands are not asked. During an interview, Quatro is forced to formulate a sharply bifurcated role, which probably rarely reflects the reality, even with the nanny she takes with her on tour: "I can't be a 24 hour a day mum or I would not be Suzi Quatro. My public gets all of me, and when I'm with my children they get all of me" (248).

In this sample are rock moms who did not conflate a rock career with pregnancy, birth, and new mothering. Viv Albertine, founding member of the Slits, experiences marriage and new motherhood in exile from her rock 'n' roll identity. Albertine in her memoir writes of a husband who did the opposite of pushing her into rock mothering, but what he does is just as abusive: "Husband never wanted me to talk about the Slits" (2014, 317). Alienated in an English beachside town, the protracted dissolution of her marriage is what seems to create space for Albertine to make—or claw—her way back to music, which she has lost her confidence for—and she is surprised that anyone remembers her or the Slits. Her coming back into this essential identity is partially incited by a male fan, *Brown Bunny* actor Vincent Gallo, who sends her a letter based on her past fame, and reminds Albertine of her essential identity: "Viv, *do* something" (319). During a trip to New York to see the New Slits, featuring some of the original band members, Albertine, with Vincent Gallo, randomly spots Patti Smith, the person around which Albertine had her '70s-era band epiphany. Back in England, Albertine, now a middle-aged "mum," buys a guitar, and starts from scratch, performing two-song sets at awkward open mics she makes six-hour round trips to play, always putting her family duties first: "Before I leave the house, I make sure my husband and daughter are fed, that she's put to bed, and that I've done the washing up" (346). Albertine's herculean efforts to be a wife and mother and return to music frustrates her husband, whose ultimatum is: "Give up music or that's it" (355). In spite of a bout of self-derision in response, Albertine, long the dutiful wife and mother, writes a paragraph that dramatically undercuts previous assertions here of the ability to do both well, and that to focus on one's own musicking, when the stakes on both sides are high—to find one's essential self this way again—is to be "unmotherly": "I do something very unmotherly now, even though it feels as though I'm losing my daughter for the second time. I don't stop concentrating on my music. I collect her from school, I make dinner, I put her to bed—I don't tidy up, I don't have time [. . .] To make this huge step I have to immerse myself in my work" (356). Unlike Quatro, Albertine finds no way to be "good at multitasking" (Quatro, 238).

What Quatro doesn't mention about multitasking is that it often means folding oneself into places of mother guilt. While Rigby has transcendent moments of folding solo mothering into musicking—bringing daughter Hazel with their band to circulate on and around the stage for an important gig at the Beacon Theatre (2019, 236), Rigby admits to many instances of mother guilt, from putting "my kid in front of the tv so I could finish a song" (203), to "feeling like the worst mother in the world" after calling home while recording new music across the country and hearing from her husband that their daughter "was just upset and really wanted you." Writes Rigby, "I was so busy with pursuing my own interests, working on my record, that I hadn't been in touch with my daughter for three days" (304). In choosing to include these moments in *Girl to City*, Rigby references the extreme vulnerability that characterizes the rock mom memoir, the mother shame that's revealed. The labor of caring for a child while trying to fulfill rock tour duties catches up with both mother and daughter. Rigby writes unflinchingly that in the club: "[. . .] I had seen Hazel with dark circles under her eyes, looking disheveled, chewing on Sue's industrial-sized key ring that always ended up in her mouth during squirmy moments and thought: 'Shouldn't we be home making craft projects with clay and pipe cleaners?'" (267). After overhearing someone say, "Who would bring a child to a place like this?" Rigby's rock mom nadir is losing her toddler at Athens, Georgia's famed 40 Watt Club: "She was all over the club, calling Mommy" (267–68). Chrissie Hynde's words to Pat Benatar are resonant here. Benatar, noting that Hynde was six months ahead of her in the "mom department," [. . .] "would have some good advice or insight":

"How are you doing this?" I asked in desperation.

"I'm not doing it! I'm *not doing it*! I'm just trying to get through the day– every day!"

(Benatar, 2010, 161)

Ford's rock mom nadir was losing access to her two sons due to parental alienation. If there was a path to this point, it may have been leaving her music career (and most of her guitars [216]) to follow a controlling husband out of the country to Turks and Caicos. Writes Ford, "I firmly hid the fact that I was miserable, living in such an isolated, dirty, and lonely place" (2016, 220). Homeschooling and caring for her two sons become her focus, as her music identity recedes (221–22). Foregrounding the complex stance of motherhood,

Ford's "only joy or pleasure" was her sons; at the same time, however, she acutely misses her connection to the music industry: " . . . it made me sad my kids had no real connection to the world I loved" (223). Eventually she attempts to conflate the two worlds: "I decided to teach James and Rocco about the 'School of Rock.' I started with the first letter of the alphabet: A is for AC/DC or Alice Cooper" (223). It's not enough. Ford reports "becoming a shadow of who [she] once was" (226). After centering her children for years, Ford needs to center herself: "But it was a Band-Aid over a hole in my heart. If music made the world go round, I ached to contribute my note" (223). Ford's epiphany at this point could be said to be her former heavy metal self: "I would Google 'Lita Ford' on my laptop and look at my old videos and interviews, trying to recover my identity. 'Lita Ford,' I missed her. I wanted her back!" (237). In recovering that former identity, Ford believed she would also save her sons: "It became clear to me . . . I needed to get away from my marriage and off that damn island. I needed to do something that made me feel like Lita again" [. . .] I had to save myself and my boys" (227). But the gamble of filing for divorce in 2010, resulted in losing her boys. According to Ford, her husband turned her sons against her. Along with music, educating others about "parental alienation" becomes a cause (230): "Lost and alone, I turned to the only thing that would give me solace: music. During the divorce proceedings, I started playing guitar again and writing songs" (231). Ford's narrative portrays the extreme vacillation of rock motherhood. Music performance requires one to center oneself; motherhood is a radically decentering project. While Ford points out her desperation to get back to the music scene after twenty years absence, on the next page she writes that she "would give up all the money in the world to be able to hold my boys in my arms" (234–35). Indie rocker Rigby amplifies this struggle, writing: "I loved being a mom, doing the things my mother had done. [. . .] But I still wanted to achieve something of my own . . . reassure myself it was okay to do work I was good at, even if it didn't help pay the bills and presented more problems than benefits for the family" (Rigby 2019, 248–49).

Tina Turner really tries to do both, but the structure of her situation doesn't allow her the choice to "multitask." She begins her career married to a controlling and abusive Ike Turner, who was infamous for his abuse and control. As a Black act touring through the pre–Civil Rights era United States, Turner must also be concerned with the threats part and parcel of structural racism. Unlike Rigby's free-wheeling tours with Hazel, where the Boston club's stage manager runs out for baby formula (Rigby, 2019, 233), for Turner, a product of pre-feminist culture and a Jim Crow South, the boundaries are very strictly drawn. Unlike Benatar, Gordon, Rigby, et al., she doesn't have the privilege of bringing baby Craig on the road with her, leaving him "in St. Louis with a sitter" (Turner 2018, 45). Turner's mother guilt stems from the fact that multitasking is not even a choice and her partner, Ike Turner, does not even allow her to "mother" when she's in a mothering space: "On our return trip cross-country, we passed through St. Louis to check on Craig, who was still living with a sitter at Ike's house. It broke my heart to see him. He was so little that he barely knew how to talk. All my son wanted was to sit in my lap, but Ike wouldn't let him" (2018, 51).

Turner laments how much they are away from the four sons she and Ike share. The boys are watched by a housekeeper (2018, 56, 80), and when the parents are home, Turner feels like she needs to protect them from "Ike's demons" that "fostered a climate of fear and uncertainty that affected the boys" (243). "I had to be both a mother and a father to them because Ike was not the kind of man to care about being a good father" (81). When they are older Turner regrets that her "Tina Turner image was a problem for them. They wished their mother could be like other mothers, and here I was, an R&B, rock 'n' roll singer and dancer, known for being a little raunchy on stage." She tries to make up for it by being the opposite with them at home: "very strict and proper" and "I never allowed them to curse or use slang" (81).

Turner's guilt is actually grief about what her first born Craig suffered because of her rock mom life and her lack of control over it. After mental health struggles, Craig commits suicide at the age of fifty-nine when Turner is seventy-eight. She writes, "I can still see him as a little boy . . . wanting so badly to sit with me when I came home from a tour, but being told to go to his room. . . . his sense of loss when I couldn't be with him. It wasn't my choice. It was the way we made our living. *Mother always gone*" (2018, 180).

While Turner seems to link her rock mom life to Craig's suicide, there is a thread running throughout these memoirs that despite the seemingly insurmountable forces that work against the enterprise, rock mothering is a necessary act that might indeed influence the child positively. Gordon attends a performance of her daughter's high school band and notes her own influence in a poignant, uncanny passage: "The voice as familiar and reminiscent of my own. The girl was my 16-year-old daughter. My daughter was fearless in her non-singer punk style that haunted me like a song I couldn't recall" (2015, 239).

Bassist Rose Simpson, of the '60s-era Incredible String Band, writes in her 2021 music memoir that a "woman's story [. . .] is more visceral, sometimes more homely and aware of its own vulnerability" (9). This statement could be applied to moments in all of the memoirs here and describes Albertine's return to the stage after a twenty-five-year break from music. In 2009, she plays a solo show at the Knitting Factory, a modestly sized Brooklyn rock club, perfect for the return of an under-the-radar rock mom. Sleater Kinney guitarist Carrie Brownstein was there. In the following excerpt from her transcendent review of this show, Brownstein elucidates the limits placed on middle-aged women when it comes to self-expression, and in the process underscores the raw power and necessary vulnerability of Albertine's comeback performance:

> If there is a voice in music that's seldom heard, it's that of a middle-aged woman singing about the trappings of motherhood, traditions and marriage. A woman who isn't trying to please or nurture anyone, but who instead illuminates a lifestyle that's so ubiquitous as to be rendered nearly invisible. She places in front of you [. . .] an image of the repressive side of domesticity, the stifling nature of the mundane, and turns every comfort and assumption you hold on its head. It raises questions that no one wants to ask a wife or a mother. [. . .] Are you happy? Was I enough? What are you sacrificing, and are those sacrifices worth it? And when someone is brave enough–honest enough–to confront the difficulty of it all, the strange, often irreconcilable dichotomy of being a mother and an artist [. . .] frankly it's scary as hell. It makes people uncomfortable. And this sentiment of unease, especially coming from a woman in her 50s sounds somewhat silly, even juvenile. Why? Because after a certain point, we're supposed to feel settled, or at the very least resigned. [. . .] it's shocking when an older woman gets on stage and basically says: This way of living and of being did not work, and the comfort that we all strive for was barely a comfort for me at all. (Brownstein 2009)

To dovetail with the mention of "trappings" above, any contemporary discussion of mothering takes place against a backdrop of "intensive mothering." As a result of interviews with thirty-eight mothers of preschool aged children, writer and researcher Sharon Hays coined the term "intensive mothering." Conflated with "good child-rearing," "intensive mothering" is realized as an encompassing persistent labor: "nurturing the child, listening to the child, attempting to decipher the child's needs and desires, struggling to meet the child's wishes, and placing the child's well-being ahead of their [mothers'] own convenience" (Christopher 2012, 75). The women of these memoirs challenge this model in a variety of ways. For them, and most working mothers, it's a model that works only intermittently. These memoirs foreground the fact that motherhood is not a monolith, nor is the experience of rock moms. In these cases, we've seen a movement where sometimes the mother is centered. As children come into their own, this becomes more possible: Turner recognizes that post divorce from Ike, in debt, that her career needs revising and reviving, and she's direct about what is required to accomplish this career goal: "I need a manager. I need a record company. I need records. And I want to fill halls like the Rolling Stones and Rod Stewart" (2018, 116). Turner takes the show "more rock and roll" (118), explaining that the "marker of a good show is freedom" (117).

To circle back to Brownstein's review, centering oneself, embracing a pre-mothering passion, may be the best iteration of mothering. Writes Albertine, "To see your mother sit down and learn an instrument from scratch, write songs, and eventually be up on stage singing them is a fantastic lesson in making your dream come true" (355). Rigby wrestles with this same notion at the conclusion of her own memoir: "Was it unfair to choose my happiness over hers, and would she understand and forgive me one day?" (306).

Musicking for themselves is essential for the very survival of these mothers. The music rock moms make is a conduit to a full sense of self, parallel to any socially constructed imperatives of what a good mother should be. Perhaps a good mother, after all, is simply the result of being a "free"—to reference Turner, the Queen Mother of Rock 'n' Roll—fully realized human being, albeit one who rocks. And so we end with Albertine's acknowledgment of this crucial space that she finally makes her way back to: "At last there is an unknown element back in my life. This is how it used to be. [. . .] I was spontaneous, free, even reckless. Things often didn't work out, but I felt alive. Painfully alive. For the last few years, I've been feeling painfully dead" (2014, 327).

Chapter 4

Vigilante Motherhood

The Embrace of Anger

> Women's anger is usually disparaged in virtually all arenas, except for those in which anger confirms gender-role stereotypes about women as nurturers and reproductive agents. This means we are allowed to be angry but not on our own behalf.
>
> (Chemaly 2018, xvii)

JOAN'S INSIGHTS

Voicing our rage as women automatically defies conventions of gender norms. A constant need for mothers to prioritize the needs of their children and others, over their own, becomes a detriment to self-care and well-being. We learn to resign ourselves to inaction, docility, and silence. For men, anger is perceived as a right and a form of authority in which the patriarchy thrives. It allows the patriarchy to control and engender emotions. All women live under the threat of violence of men—that is the power structure that we live in. To voice our rage and anger wars with deep-seated and internalized misogyny, often a complicated concept to unpack. "56 percent of American men think sexism has been eradicated from American Life" (Chemaly 2018, 224). Self-silencing rage is normalized by women as well.

I recall one particular Friday morning when I was driving my girls to school and daycare. It was supposed to be a good day—last day of the week, what my kids often called *Fri-yay*, where we switch off and they get to be with their dad for the weekend. Unbeknownst to me, I didn't realize all the subconscious stress that had been bubbling under the surface of my functional and cheerful adulting exterior. The week had started out with facility issues at my library, and I was struggling to get my custody and visitation documents squared away with my ex, who was difficult with communication and, yet again, making me deal with the labor of our ending marriage. I recall trying to let the little things go so I could get through the week—socks I saw under the ottoman (I'd get them later, I told myself), needing to buy a new thermos for my daughter, planning her upcoming birthday, and so on. Did I schedule their annual checkups yet? What are we going to have for dinner tonight? Would my little one even eat the leftovers for lunch tomorrow? I have to run out and get more shampoo. Is it too much to ask my parent friend to do all the pick-ups this week? How am I going to juggle the after-work event and the kids this Thursday?

Skip back to that particular Friday in the car with my girls. We're stuck in traffic at the drop-off point by my older daughter's school and both the girls start fighting in the backseat, and I mean screaming-fighting in the backseat over an Encanto song of all things.

I remember the facade of my face just crumbling under the weight of the unresolved and untapped stress that had built to this very moment. I was in some surreal vacuum of space in my car, watching the children cross with the crossing guard, the parents laughing with their kids and holding hands as they moved along the street. The visuals just taunted my inner battle of maintaining a calm facade for my kids and myself when all I wanted to do was scream. I thought of rage, the ways in which pain and anger are minimized and dismissed because I happen to have a vagina. That men are allowed to embrace this one emotion publicly rather than confront the spectrum of emotions we all experience.

In that moment, I exploded. I don't remember my exact words, but I know I bellowed with something like "*Just be quiet!*," turned off the radio, gripped the steering wheel, and cried with rage and yes, a little sadness. The girls quieted immediately. And I was saddened by the fact that they had never witnessed a mother who didn't allow the emotion of anger. It cemented to me that as mothers, we rarely do.

> Coping often involves self-silencing and feelings of powerlessness. Getting anger out in this way is not the same as envisioning anger as a transitional tool that helps you to change the world around you. (Chemaly 2018, xiii)

This self-silencing and lack of agency were common patterns exhibited by our musical moms. It became a fascinating space for us to explore how rock and metal moms in particular navigated and coped with the dualities of good/bad mothering and their own empowerment as musicians performing in heavily white male spaces. The mothers who were musicians often spoke on how liberating it was to perform, to live in an empowering space in which they could let go, breathe, feel real and have agency. It was an understanding of this space as a place in which they could fight back.

What resulted were mothers who returned to spheres in which they could exact their agency—oftentimes identifying themselves in musical genres already transgressive for women and their participation—in our case, rock, punk, and metal. As scholar Bertolini has stated, this aligns the women in our study with the vigilante women in fiction that Bertolini has written about and like D'Amore's analysis of fictional female characters, our participants fulfilled the same three moral criteria (Bertolini 2011, 21):

1. She identifies the wrong that has been done to her and recognizes her lack of legal recourse for retribution.
2. She determines how she can respond with punishment that fits the crime.
3. She determines that she has herself a moral authority to enforce sanctions, because no one else is willing or able to act in her place.

This idea of a vigilante mother or avenger allowed our participants to resist and combat structures of patriarchal oppression. Their simple existence in these musical spheres become acts of retribution through presence, representation, and lyrical compositions. Their embodied performances on stage creates a counter to the male hegemony inherent in their musical genres.

In addition, voice, in its literal sense, becomes a tool and vehicle of agency for these women to disrupt the social order of the punk and metal subcultures. In metal, female vocalists who stylistically perform in male-coded behaviors (i.e., death growls, screams, Cookie Monster vocals)[1] disrupt the overall masculine space. As scholar Karen Eileraas notes, this type of performativity serves as a form of *ugliness*, a resistance practice in music (Eileraas 1997, 122). What we bear witness to are defiant women who are intentional in both their appearance and performance within their genres, as cited by our interviewee below:

> But I'm loud, I'm clumsy, I'm messy. I have opinions. I have emotions. Our society doesn't tolerate that in women. Punk rock was the acceptable way to be that way. As a woman who has always been told I'm "too much." (Julie Unruly)

This direct and self-aware acknowledgment from our participants offers a space of catharsis and liminality. It is uncensored, raw, and conceptualized from an authentic mothered experience. The *ugliness* counters language itself, especially when applied through vocal expressions like screaming. The women rebel against the etiquette of acceptable and pretty behavior. Instead, engaging in this punk and metal way aids in dismantling the male hegemony of performance and disrupts gender. This was essential for our interviewees' ability to create a self that was independent of "good" mothering practices. Combined with *ugliness*, vigilante motherhood gives agency to these mother-performers, empowering them in self-made spaces, allowing them to compete on equal terms with their male counterparts.

While we would think that vigilante mother-performers would only convey or embody this ugliness, the juxtaposition inherently encoded in black metal music lends itself to creating a wonderfully liminal space where mother-performers can exist and convey a sense of beauty built on their musical compositions. One example of this can be seen through the black metal performer—Myrkur (Amalie Bruun) hailing from Denmark who builds upon typical black metal music characteristics and yet combines a softer contextual concept of the topics she chooses to perform. In a 2020 interview for *The Line of Best Fit*, Myrkur writes:

> You give your entire life, and yourself all of a sudden, because you are just a house for a foetus. And as beautiful as that is, you have to almost kill a part of yourself to get through that. (Kelly 2020)

This concept of suffering in order to bring birth to life is definitely not an uncommon one for many women. It was cited often by our participants that a true life/work balance was not possible, and motherhood became an identity that either was wholly adopted into one's new self, or temporarily adopted as a retreat from their musical identity that held more autonomy and power. Patriarchal conventions and societal norms were often to blame in an era of parenting books that cited acceptable mothering roles. For those mothers who were able to masterly blend the soft with the hard (in this case rock and metal lives) with their role as mothers, these lives manifested in several ways—mothers who accepted being transgressive mothers (imperfect from society's measures), mothers who retreated, however brief or long from the rock 'n' roll lifestyle, and mothers who found other outlets from their musical roots, often channeling their creative endeavors into more acceptable activities. However, from our study, many women cited the strong pull of music and its importance to their identities as mothers—an area of empowerment they could not dismiss or ignore.

Mothering and suffering come about in several ways and initially can simply arise from the work needed to even become a mother. Motherhood as the ideal escalator of a marriage and the next steps to starting a family can bring about a plethora of challenges. Rita Sembuya (2010), founder of the Joyce Fertility Support Centre in Uganda, writes, "Our culture demands that, for a woman to be socially acceptable, she should have at least one biological child, and . . . In many cultures, childless women suffer discrimination, stigma and ostracism." Such pressures on women combine extreme anxiety and agony when faced with infertility issues. The costs associated with testing, IVF treatment, the maintenance with egg harvesting or surrogacy all add up. The role of good mothering and self-sacrifice persist through class and ethnicity. This ideology only reinforces the gender inequalities that lie in the conventional family structure. Women get the "shit end of the stick," so to speak. The tendency for women to take on the emotional labor and work, while managing the pragmatic functions of a household and working fulltime is often dismissed as part and parcel of a women's duty. Male musicians don't get asked how they're going to handle touring while having a family—it's a default that the wife or partner will handle this challenge. And while there are husbands and partners that approach this work more equitably, it is certainly not the default. Again, participants cited the guilt they felt having to leave their children while on tour or to take them along, but not give them the stable environment of children their age. These women's concerns seemed antithetical to what they really wanted for their families and could not achieve as rock and metal moms.

NOTE

1. "Extremely deep, throaty growling, often sounds muddier, less articulate than mid- or high pitched growling" (Ritlop 2020, 150).

Chapter 5

Daughters on Rock Moms

Life, Performance, Musicking, and Bonding

The focus of the work gathered here has been on mothers instead of their children, who conventionally get all the attention. We have chosen this focus as a necessary corrective and addition to scholarly conversations on high intensity motherhood, a neoliberal project defined by ensuring one's children obtain skills—music skills among these—that make them competitive in a capitalist framework. Our gaze has been on "mothers who rock," with their children as the afterthought, merely alluded to, implied. But mothers don't mother in a vacuum. In the case of Patti Smith who routinely performs with her millennial daughter, Jesse Paris on keyboards, and sometimes with her son, Jackson, some mothers don't rock without them either. And of course there is a relatively long history of mothers and daughters performing together in country music, the Judds, the Carter Family, among these. But what is the experience of the child taking in a mother's art? Viewing the mother as the contextually centered and aberrational rock 'n' roller?

These questions formed after a viewing of the 2021 feature-length documentary *Poly Styrene: I Am a Cliche* on the English punk legend Poly Styrene, born as Marianne Joan Elliott-Said (Waters 2015, 161). Styrene was the creative force behind the ephemeral, yet wildly influential post-punk band X-Ray Spex: the band's captivating front person, vocalist, lyricist, and future mother of Celeste Bell. Bell, who wrote, directed, and narrated the documentary, foregrounds within that the documentary is not just a conventional tracing of a life, but also a daughter's essential search for who her mother was before she became a mother. Bell lends shape and a poignant perspective to her mother's journey, from a disenfranchised biracial girl in a racially bifurcated Brixton, England, to a visionary and iconic punk rocker during the apex of the British scene, to a bipolar mother and Krishna devotee. At documentary's end, Bell brings her mother's story back, redemptively, to music when Poly Styrene performs powerfully at the Roundhouse just before her breast cancer diagnosis. In the film's opening, Bell establishes that this journey into her mother's life will be complex for her, even painful. Being raised by a sensitive, creative genius, diagnosed with bi-polar disorder, meant that Bell often suffered under her mother's care, or lack thereof (Bell and Sng 2021). In the oral history *Dayglo: The Poly Styrene Story*, published before the film's release, Bell frames Styrene's complex story as one of a problematic mother, whose cumulative effect on Bell she is still unpacking: "People often ask me if she was a good mum. It's always a hard question to answer. [. . .] She was an artist, a maverick, an individual, an eccentric. [. . .] She also struggled, as so many creative geniuses do, with mental health issues. Do such characters make good parents? I suppose it depends on what we mean by 'good parents.' Dependable, responsible, stable, organized? Nope. Not in my experience" (2019, 7).

Like mothers we interviewed, surveyed, studied, and enjoyed here, Styrene, a nineteen-year-old woman of color in a white male–dominated music scene, built her music identity and career before Bell was born. Liminally positioned, an outsider in terms of race, neither Black nor white, Styrene's fascination with the theme of identity is no surprise. The tribalism of identity, the pull and horror of it, is realized in "Identity," her song written for X-Ray Spex (Goldman 2019, 19). Its excruciating lyrics include: "When you see yourself / Does it make you scream?" (Styrene 1978). After Bell is born, Styrene departs the band that brought her international attention, critical acclaim, and a spot in the punk pantheon. Styrene makes a couple of ignored and/or critically panned solo albums, during which she becomes a mother. Dropped from her label, Syrene leaves Bell with her father and joins up with the Hare Krishnas (Bell and Sng 2021). Styrene seemed intent on leaving the identity that made her famous and memorable behind forever. To reference a lyric from the song, Styrene "smashed it quick," but in doing so, Styrene was doing nothing to fulfill "good mothering" imperatives: On the contrary, after some time with her mother at the Krishna ashram in England, Bell moves in with her grandmother at the age of eight. This chapter's exposition sets up the emotional heart of the film: despite Styrene's failings as a mother that extend over her daughter's life, it is the mother's circling back to musicking participation—her essential identity—at the age of fifty-one that incites a seeming reconciliation between mother and daughter. In 2008, Styrene, with a new band arrayed around her, emerges to give a triumphant performance at the famed Roundhouse in London, the emotional core of the film, in our opinion. Witnessing the adoring, passionate crowd, those who waited decades for her return, and those who discovered X-Ray Spex in Styrene's absence, is deeply moving. Styrene's return to the stage takes the form of a healing and redemptive moment between a troubled mother and neglected daughter, and Bell, after meticulous and protracted research through her mother's archives, tracing a path through so many of her mother's identities, viscerally witnesses who her mother was and is. That moment—a daughter's epiphany, if you will—is the reason this chapter exists. In the footage, we see Bell giddy with her mother on stage for the encore, one that features X-Ray Spex's signature song "Oh Bondage! Up Yours!" Bell joins in on the chorus and dances with her mother in a frenzy, making her active participation in Styrene's redemption her own: a young adult now, Bell seems to be musicking the trauma wrought by a bipolar mother away, or at least keeping it a bay for a while. The vision of mother and daughter at least visually reconciled on stage is exuberant, and exuberance was always Styrene's secret weapon (Waters 2015, 161). At fifty-one, not long before she's diagnosed with metastatic breast cancer, mama Styrene is still a force—the signature energy she generates that emanates from the screen in Bell's film is breathtaking. "She kicked ass up there," Bell reminisces to the camera with unmitigated joy and pride (Bell and Sng 2021).

Styrene's English punk colleague and fellow "mum" Viv Albertine has a similar musicking and mothering trajectory. Like Styrene, Albertine is a key part of a critically acclaimed band that explodes onto the same tiny London scene. And similar to Styrene's story, when the band recedes, Albertine does, too. Finally, Albertine's rock mom-and-redemption story also draws its power from finding an essential musicking identity again, seemingly against all odds. When Albertine gathers enough confidence, after a protracted hiatus, to sit in with the New Slits on guitar, she takes her daughter Vida out of school to attend the show. Unlike in Styrene's story, where the redemptive moment is narrated by the daughter, Vida's point of view is given to the reader via Albertine in her 2014 memoir: "I only need to look down from the stage at her in the front row, her eyes fixed on me with a look of such glowing pride, to know that I've done the right thing for her" (Albertine 2014, 353–54). Because Styrene dies, two-and-a-half years after her Roundhouse show, we are left to wonder if Styrene would have conflated good rocking with good mothering the way Albertine does here: "To see your mother sit down and learn an instrument from scratch, write songs, and eventually be up on stage singing them is a fantastic lesson in making your dream come true" (2014, 355).

The pattern of family as a site of bonding between mother and daughter has been explored by scholar Rita Grácio in her article "Daughters of Rock and Moms Who Rock: Rock Music as a Medium for Family Relationships in Portugal" in which Gracio investigates musicking under the lens of women rockers and their daughters, referencing Christopher Small's work on musicking in family relationships (Small 1990). Here Gracio explores how mothers

Figure 5.1. Moan Elisa of the Trash Bags musicking with daughters.
Source: Photo by Lauren Krohn

impart the love of music through family experiences with their children and discusses how children often form core memories through exposure to the musical preferences of a parent. She writes on how mothers can control the initial stages of how their children are exposed to music, and how later, as the child grows, where a space of exploration can continue to help shape a child's autonomy. Not unlike our study, our participants identified childhood memories associated with both mothers and fathers imparting significant "musical memories."

One of our participants, Alexandra Velardes, a thirty-three-year-old white cisgender queer woman, writes that her core musical identity carried forth into how she practiced motherhood:

> In regard to how music coincided with motherhood . . . It was important to us (husband and wife) that music would always be a part of her (daughter's) life and I have sung to her from day one as has he. "I Will Follow You into the Dark" by Death Cab will always be her lullaby. Music has always been in my life, and I would be hard pressed to remember my earliest memory but two of my most formative ones were listening to Nanci Griffith with my mom in the car as an elementary schooler and when I was fifteen and went to my first ska/emo show at our city's local venue. The importance of Nanci Griffith was how raw her music felt. There was so much emotion in every one of her songs and I didn't truly feel that again until I was standing in The Venue of 5th and Broad. (Velardes 2022)

This bonding over music becomes a site for nostalgia and offers these mothers generational influence and memory making for their family unit. Many of our participants cited specific moments (concerts, shows, and listening experiences) as vital experiences in which they realized how much music was to become integral in their lives. Joan's own experience with heavy and extreme metal originated from hearing the death metal bands Carcass and Death during the loss of her mother when she was twenty-three. Introduced to their music earlier in life, these tones didn't resonate until she was grieving her mother. Only then did her ears appreciate the heavy down-tuned guitar playing, double bass drums and unrecognizable vocals that would emulate the pain she was enduring on the inside. In this way, through extreme music, Joan was essentially bonding with her mother, even after her mother was gone.

Additionally, the ways in which we are first exposed to music listening can have a long-lasting effect. As Mallika points out:

> The first metal acts with women I heard were Arch Enemy, Sinister, and Crisis, bands which I was exposed to through friends during those college years (post-2000). Probably the two biggest influences which brought me into the metal music scene were these. Freshman year of college, I lived down the block from a famous music club, The Middle East in Cambridge. I used to go down there with my roommate and check out shows all the time, even if we didn't know who was playing. Another thing that happened was I met some metalheads at my college, Massachusetts College of Art, who exposed me to some bands, and

also introduced me to an important local metal forum, ReturnToThePit.com. Through these outlets, I really got to know the local music scene as well as international touring acts, and I found other musicians to jam with. I was navigating these scenes as one of the only women, however, and it was very lonely a lot of the time. I would bring my younger sister and girlfriends with me to concerts and try-outs even if it wasn't their cup of tea. (Mallika 2021)

Interviewing the daughters of one of this book's authors was another way to approach this topic–an autoethnography framed by motherhood. Julie's participation in music has largely been as a fan and consumer of it, but she has performed in rock spaces post motherhood, both as a reader of her original rock 'n' roll-themed fiction and in rock performance as a vocalist with her ex-spouse, the daughter's father. The following interview took place with both daughters present: Zoë, twenty-three at the time of the interview, and Stella, twenty. Julie initiates the interview by asking them both why neither had ever attended one of her performances, assuring them that she wasn't hurt or angry by their absence, only curious.

Zoë responds as follows:

Starting in middle school, I didn't want to be seen with you in public, and that kind of went on through high school. That's a big part of why I didn't come to any performances you did. I wanted to separate myself from your lives. While in middle school, I saw Dad perform once at the Sidewalk Cafe in the East Village, and it made me feel weird seeing him perform in front of an audience. I think I was almost embarrassed, having all the attention be on him was a little weird, especially because he performed a song he wrote about Stella and me. That was also embarrassing.

Stella offers this rejoinder that undercuts Albertines' glowing assertion of the positive influence a mother performing on stage might have on a daughter:

It feels uncomfortable to be asked to watch you on stage. We have our own lives and I've been occupied with my own issues throughout my entire life. But I think anything celebrating motherhood is good and positive. Because so much of the time, society tells us that you can't be attractive and pregnant, or you can only be pregnant in a certain attractive way.

At this point in the conversation, Zoë is quick to another perspective that resides outside the boundaries of a parents' stage work:

But it's cool to be able to say both my parents are artists. It's interesting to say that when you guys first moved to New York City, Dad was trying to be a musician. It's not something you hear every day when you're a kid. Going to that Abortion Stories event with you this year at that Brooklyn club, where your friends, all those moms performed in protest of the Supreme Court's recent decision was awesome. Middle-aged moms yelling and singing and reciting poetry and stories about abortion on stage was super cool to see. Watching moms perform and take up that space and be loud, being unapologetic about themselves and their self lives. It made me think that it's important for mothers to show their complexity, share things that make their experience imperfect, different from how it's "supposed to look." That's cool to see. And it's true that women who want to have creative paths and unconventional paths are often cautioned against motherhood. They're made to feel like they can't be moms and be powerful in an artistic sense. That's what Lauryn Hill's song "To Zion" is about. It's not rock. It's R&B. Her son's name is Zion and the song is about being told her career is going to get messed up by her kid. But I think it's almost gotten cool or trendy to have a kid right now. To be like a hot, interesting pregnant person. How about just being a person? It's a double-edged thing. Public pregnancy has become more validated. Rihanna's had her belly out her whole pregnancy. It's really cool to see and she's a Black woman, pushing against the image of what a mother is, what an acceptable mother is.

Stella: "Being pregnant has become another aesthetic. What happened to just being a mother?"

Zoë: "What happened to just being a person?"

Stella: "We always have to think about mom's responsibilities. Women, in general, throughout their lives don't get their needs met and then they become moms, and they become 'martyr mothers' in a way, because they never became their own mom."

Zoë: "From what I can see, a lot of mothering becomes about sacrifice. Losing yourself and your identity."

Stella: "The point of life is to experience the multi-faceted nature of it. That's why we have children, I think. They say that being a parent is the most unselfish thing you can do, but a lot of it is selfish. You're making copies of yourself. But it's also a great thing, because connection and family can be great."

Zoë: "I feel having a child is inherently for yourself, at the end of the day. No one needs to bring a child into this world. Another life doesn't need to be created. You make the decision first of all for yourself. You don't make the decision for this theoretical new person who doesn't exist yet."

Stella: "I think there's way too much pressure put on the potential of babies. The things we project onto babies starts at birth, like gender."

Zoë then unwittingly underscores some of the essential limitations of our project, previously alluded to:

There hasn't been all that much time since gay marriage was legalized and queer couples found it easier to have family units. I think it would be good to talk to queer people about this topic, because they're already challenging so much of what the family unit and parental roles are supposed to look like. A kid being raised by two moms, or one woman and one non-binary person, that would be so different, finding out how they push back against that cis-gendered heteronormative structure.

Stella seems to agree: "These old definitions are based on a lot of toxic systems. It's based on an upper class white tradition for mothers to compete with each other. It's another story when you're talking to mothers who have been oppressed."

Despite this, Zoë seems to want the discussion to reside on a positive, affirmative note:

> But I think having an art life being validated by a parent was pretty unusual and important to me, because I took it really seriously from a young age, too. When I was younger I wanted to be an artist or a writer, and those were life or career paths that you never told me I couldn't do.

Stella: "I was never scared to study art, or pursue art, or to dress how I wanted. I think the freedom of expression that is involved in having artist parents is really cool and unique."

Julie: "I feel like I was mostly mothering, but I think what I was doing was trying to combine the two things."

Zoë: "You always read to us. You were always writing around us. Seeing your parents take art seriously makes an impact. I really remember that Sonic Youth concert you took us to in Prospect Park. I was twelve. I remember art was around us all the time. I remember spending so much time at the Met. We were there constantly. It's always been seen as extremely important, as something to take seriously. I know a lot of artists when they're younger feel like they can't take it as seriously. That they need to do something more reliable. It's a risk in this society. But I think it's the only thing that would make me happy. The potential reward is higher than the risk."

Drummer and mother Christy Davis gave our book its evocative working title *Snare Drum at My Womb*. One of the first rock moms we interviewed, Davis used this phrase in her interview to describe her particularly seamless transition from drummer to mother. In her interview, Davis reflects on the fact she sat behind a kit and drummed throughout her pregnancy, after giving birth, and into new motherhood. She collaborated with musicians, sometimes other mothers, and she has never stopped. Her daughter Stella gestated throughout her mother's drumming, the snare's sharp resonance coming

Figure 5.2. Christy Davis celebrates the success of her daughter's band on Instagram.
Source: Screenshot. Band photo by Jessica Gurewitz

through Christy to her. One might be compelled to make the connection then from this fetal space to Stella outside the womb, watching her mother practice and perform with her own bands, to the fact that Stella has herself emerged as a talented drummer for an alternative rock band with two other young women: this band Hello Mary is one about to break out. Christy's Instagram post in this chapter is from a 2022 *Rolling Stone* article: their "Artist You Need to Know" column implores us to "Say Hello to the Next Great New York Rock Band." That band is Hello Mary. While the article's focus is on the band, Davis is alluded to as the one responsible for Stella's idiosyncratic music tastes relative to Generation Z. Growing up, Stella, born in 2000, not only absorbed her mother's drummer identity, but was fed a diet of '90s alternative rock, what *Rolling Stone* terms as Davis's "parentally approved guitar weirdness." Before Davis deejayed one of Stella's elementary school dances, Stella made sure she did not disrupt it: "'You can't play your [Gen X] music. You have to play pop hits so that the kids like me'" (Vozick-Levinson 2022, para 10). Fast forward, and mother and daughter are basically on the same page when it comes to music. And Davis, who has played in bands since the '80s, has been indispensable in getting her daughter's off the ground. Davis conflates the work of musicking mothers and daughters in words she sent us, reflecting on her daughter's success in one of the toughest industries on the planet: "It's been amazing to mentor Stella's band and be interwoven into their journey by both sharing the stage with them as well as acting as tour 'momager' on various mini tours.:) My pride is indescribable." (Davis, Personal Communication, December 7, 2022)

Chapter 6

Mother Tracks

Rock and Metal Moms Write Motherhood

When a mom is mentioned in rock lyrics, she's usually kind of a drag. Any alluded to mother figure is the admonisher, reminder of boundaries—peripherally placed, an anathema to fun, or the track's internal drama. In Randy Newman's 1966 song "Mama Told Me Not to Come," famously and raucously covered by Three Dog Night in 1970, the song's central persona can't even indulge in the established "bacchanalian" scene without referencing over and over again that "Mama" had given him ample warning to stay away (Three Dog Night 1970). In Ozzy Osbourne's "Mama, I'm Coming Home," "Mama," conflated with girlfriend, is the locus of comfort and stability, synonymous with home, strength, and stasis (Osbourne 1992). "Mama" is an Odyssean Penelope in a tube top and tight jeans waiting for her ragged and yearny boyfriend, who's flailing but having all the fun. Mama keeps things safe, and a little dull. For context, it seems necessary to acknowledge that the "mother as monitor" stance seemed to reach its apex in mothers not constructed within songs, however, but in opposition to them, namely the real-life mothers of the Parents Music Resource Center (PMRC). In 1985, along with three other political and professional wives and mothers, Tipper Gore, wife of the future Vice President, discovered sexually explicit lyrics on a Prince album her then tween daughter brought home, and founded the PMRC to advocate for warning labels on records they felt needed them (Schonfed 2015). Many artists of the time who were targets of the PMRC pushed back on this iteration of "repressive mothering"—a mothering stance that went beyond the relatively measured warnings of the mother in Newman's song. Misfits' vocalist Glenn Danzig's "Mother" is somewhat of a rejoinder to the PMRC's mission. The persona of "Mother" has an intense self-consciousness about "his" own danger. It's a PMRC warning label personified. These lines from "Mother" provide advice for extreme monitor mothers everywhere: "Mother, tell your children not to walk my way / Tell your children not to hear my words" (Danzig 1988). Whether inside or outside of the song, Mothers protect children from the potential ravages of rock 'n' roll.

So what do rock 'n' roll mothers themselves write when they write about mothering? What does it look like when mothers—instead of observing, supporting, admonishing, limiting—express themselves and their own experiences over the course of a music track? What does a mother identity look like in the songs rock 'n' roll mothers write and perform? This chapter gathers and unpacks the songwriting work of rock moms when they write about motherhood: some were interviewed for this book, some are rock stars or punk icons, others write songs that mock or satirize the experience of motherhood. In addition, we will explore the idea of mothering lyrics that engage with mental states, isolation, and heavy metal music.

At first glance, the songs gathered and examined here might be said to epitomize "heavy" in the "heavy music mothering" experience: "heavy" as in "heavy laden" with care. Many of these artists cast the experience of motherhood as, at times, burdensome, problematic, fraught. These rock moms' songs are laced with heavy issues, ranging from mild marital unease to mothering ennui, to parent/child estrangement. Indeed, the mother lyricist has attempted to represent and amplify an authentic motherhood experience, sadness and all, as opposed to an idealized one. Furthermore, a PMRC-style reproachful mother identity is subverted when mothers themselves are the source of the narrative trouble in the lyrics. For example, Liz Phair's "Little Digger" is a song written in first person wherein the aberrational persona addresses a son catching her—his mother—with "another guy" (Phair 2003).

If not aberration and disruption, there's an abundant amount of resignation and heartache being constructed in mother tracks. New York–based rocker and singer/songwriter Amy Rigby's 1996 album *Diary of a Mod Housewife*—a riff on the 1967 Sue Kaufman novel about the demise of a loveless marriage with children, *Diary of a Mad Housewife*—movingly chronicles the mundanity of marriage and motherhood, the tensions and subtle aggressions. Rigby's record, created and released when album tracks were arranged to build stories from track to track, slings the slog into tuneful arrangements. The lyrics reference admonishing looks, the annoyance at the edge of a voice in "That Tone of Voice," to drunken marital fights: "I've got bruises on my knees" from "Didn't I." In "Sad Tale," the fractured couple are so estranged they "raise their kid over the telephone." In the track "Beer and Kisses" the couch, no doubt broken-down, is a grim all night locus for the couple who "grew a little couch potato / You said she looked just like me," intimating that the pattern of dysfunction nailed in the phrase "Get home from work, get in a fight" is likely to be passed down. Yet, the album's final track, "We're

Stronger Than That" is cautiously hopeful. The first lyric line reminds the weary spouse of the couple's marital vows, the robustness of early marriage, and its natural decline: "Shattered hopes / tired jokes," The song's persona, injects the line: "Baby, we're stronger than that." The enervation of child rearing is referenced: "We're stronger than the fairy tails, diaper pails" and then there is an almost breathtaking segue into hints of future infidelity: "Lack of heat, urge to cheat." The track's final line comes after succumbing to the chronicling of the mundane. Life, no matter how rock 'n' roll the couple: "tv shows, runny nose" is a phrase resigned to the tedium. In stark contrast to the escapist fantasies embodied in KISS tracks wherein rock stars are impervious to age and tedium, asserting a Raymond Carver–esque mundane is perhaps the most rock 'n' roll element of all, and the most valuable takeaway of the rock mom track.

Rigby's assertion of the quotidian, the tedium of motherhood could be said to exist alongside the most poignant, broken "lost in the bottle" George Jones tune. But in Jones's case, the source of suffering is detachment from the love object, the deflation of romance, and escape into the tedium of the bottle. In listening to and scanning the lyrics of these mother tracks, does the rhetoric of suffering make for the best art or at least the most interesting iteration of motherhood in a rock context? There is no death wish here. On the contrary, a tenacity in the face of the slog, a commitment to follow through.

Post-punk icon and rock mom Viv Albertine, of the legendary English band the Slits, released a solo album in 2012. This album *The Vermillion Border* contains tracks explicit in their problematic relationship to motherhood. Whereas Rigby alludes to motherhood tangentially, disjunctively contextualizing marriage and motherhood with wry and lovely rhymes, Albertine's iteration is stark and raw. Yet like Rigby's, Albertine's is an intensely personal and autobiographical album; both are essentially memoirs set to music.

Indeed, both Albertine's and Rigby's mother tracks seem directly channeled from life, and in doing so obliquely reference their respective published memoirs. In *Girl to City*, Rigby details meeting her husband and the father of her child, drummer for the dB's, Will Rigby. Like her spouse, Rigby was and is an active indie rocker, who never put her guitar down with marriage and motherhood. In stark contrast, in Albertine's memoir *Clothes, Clothes, Clothes, Music, Music, Music, Boys, Boys, Boys*, Albertine details her twenty-five-year break from active musicking as a guitar player and songwriter after the demise of the Slits. During the break, she physically leaves the site of her musicking and fame, moving from London to the suburban English coast. How she reclaims her identity is the narrative's heart, reconfigured in the mother tracks presented here. To describe her return to music is to imagine a woman "clawing her way back" in ways physical and emotional. For one, Albertine has to teach herself how to play the guitar again. Her 2014 memoir describes how, newly determined, Albertine brings her guitar everywhere to practice—as long as it's out of range of her disapproving husband, even playing in the car while waiting to collect her daughter. Albertine's journey, coming on the heels of a life-threatening cancer battle, is arduous. Yet at the time of her comeback album's release, Albertine, a nearly fifty-eight-year-old single mother, is focused, determined, motivated (Albertine 2014). Overcoming what seems like a fortress of impediments, Albertine takes possession of her musicking self again. This return to an essential identity, is now overlain with marriage and motherhood, and she has different things to say. Her midlife musicking iteration comes to the listener in the stark lyrics of two mother-referencing tracks from her full-length solo debut.

"Confessions of a MILF"[1] wastes no time laying out the situation at hand. The stark, urgent lyrics underscore that Albertine, after a lifetime of silence, simply has no time to waste. The cushions of literary metaphor are all but absent here. "Confessions" is a general indictment of marriage from the wife's point of view. While the song opens with the repeated refrain, "Home sweet home," "Mama's" home is not "homey." The lyrics in this section are spiked, nervous, and staccato. While motherhood is only referenced by the "M" in the title, the lyrics, like Rigby's, paint a landscape of insipid domestic imperatives—an onslaught, truthfully: peeling potatoes, drizzling the lemon cake, retrieving the biscuits, presumably for tea. There is no gentle segue from this into the persona's indictment of her unsupportive husband. "You are not a god," Albertine addresses "him," her vocals here breathy, desperate. The remainder of the lyrics construct the persona/wife's total disillusionment with the idea of romantic love and marriage; the choice to marry disrupts any personal sense of security. There is no tranquility in this domestic scene. In the following lines, we realize that Albertine is the song's persona. Life informs art with no alteration: "I chose being an artist over being a wife. Now I'm gonna lead a very lonely life" (lines 40, 42). After interrupting the narrative with more anxious repetition, the persona asserts her home has become a locus of alienation: "Don't make me go home, 'cause I hate my home." As opposed to Rigby's quiet resignations when describing marital life, Albertine's energy in "Confessions" makes it impossible to settle in. The tone references the angular punk aesthetic that defined Albertine's defiant guitar work for the Slits, back when girls were not meant to be heard. Jettisoning decades forward, Albertine in late middle age is ready to flail again. Fifty-something MILFs are also meant to be heard: "no peace in my home, no faith . . . no love in my home," and in perhaps, an oblique reference to punk progenitor, Iggy Pop, "no fun in my home."

"IVF," the other "mother track" on *The Vermillion Border* is as nakedly autobiographical. Albertine's real life grueling IVF journey eventually resulted in the birth of her only child, Vida in 1999 (Albertine 2014). The track's figurative language is disturbing, even macabre, and lingers on bodies and babies as commodities, factory products: "pretty babies, tied up with bows," "piles of babies," "miles of babies," and then the phrase "light bruises" is recontextualized, each repetition set in a pastoral, surreal context that could be decidedly "black metal": "Twisting forest" in which "nothing fills the void," the persona who runs with "no legs." The forest is left behind and the point of view, over the course of five recast related lyric lines, assumes a singularity of focus on a body in crisis—visibly bruised. The bruises are described at first as aesthetically pleasing: "light bruises on white flesh," but quickly shifts to the disturbing and dramatic, "Fucked up with light bruises." The track concludes with a concentration of nihilistic lines. What's written creates a landscape of alienation and obliteration: "Slipping down, down, down / Into unconsciousness" (Albertine 2014).

What has emerged up to now in this discussion of rock women writing motherhood are portraits of mothers writing along a range of anguish, suffering, and discombobulation. From this survey so far, when rock moms write about motherhood, the experience can be interpreted as troubled, uncomfortable, trapped, and even tragic, as in the case of Lita Ford's "Mother" from her 2012 album *Living Like a Runway* (Ford 2016). Founding member and lead guitarist of the legendary all girl band the Runaways, Ford *is* the mother of "Mother." Readers of Ford's 2016 memoir *Living Like a Runway* will know there is no meaningful separation between the persona of the song and "Lita," the real-life rock mom. Ford is direct about this in her memoir, "I wrote a new song on the album called 'Mother' for my kids" (2016, 238). "The song explains parental alienation, because I want my kids to know what happened" (2016, 238).

In "Mother," Ford's gut-wrenching power ballad, she disrupts the genre's usual tropes. Instead of a blighted adult romance, "Mother" is about a radically disrupted mother/child relationship, and the song opens with one of the two direct assertions of motherhood in this discussion: "I am your mother." That established, the lyrics acknowledge that the relationship—this primal bond—has been seemingly irrevocably damaged—Ford has been cut off from her two sons. In the accompanying music video that features Ford performing the song in what seems to be Joshua Tree, California, edited with footage of young boys who could be her sons, Ford performs "Mother" with an expression of agony that seems genuinely felt, rupturing, for a moment, the signature toughness of her usual performance persona. The music video for "Mother" can be considered a signature rock mom document. The entirety of the track is one of profound regret about the fracturing of the family and an impassioned apology to her two sons. From Ford's point of view, the father of her children willfully, spitefully turned them against her ("A Metal Mother's Day Chat" 2012). Ford's tone in "Mother" is unflinching and nakedly honest, direct: "I am your mother / Please understand why I had to leave / Pain was deep / He was hurting me" (Ford, Track 6). The song ends poignantly, with an assertion of the essential mother/child bond, even within a landscape of enormous loss: "I'll always be your mother / I'll always be a part of you."

Ford is, as of this writing, still largely estranged from the two sons—children that she abandoned her music career to raise. Like Albertine, Ford essentially cuts herself—or allows herself to be cut off from her music career—in order to follow her husband and sons off beaten paths. Given Ford's usual rock role as a renowned heavy metal guitar shredder, it's a startling song in its centering of a mother's love and regret. And like Albertine's, Ford's lyrics here veer into the realm of black metal, a genre that seems to be the most appropriate container.

The epitome of the suffering mother in Judeo-Christian culture is the goddess Mary, mother of Jesus. The thirteenth-century Latin hymn "Stabat Mater," or "Suffering Mother," is the story of Mary's suffering at the site of Jesus's crucifixion. Alongside her son, the god on the cross, Mary suffers epically, and the persona of "Stabat Mater" seems awestruck by it, even a little envious—getting to Christ through Mary's suffering is the goal. But unlike the other mother rockers here, Mary has no voice in this track. Her thoughts on this scene are projected onto her by the narrating voice of the hymn. On her suffering, she is mute, silently bereft at the scene. The hymn has been

Figure 6.1. Lita Ford in music video for "Mother."
Source: Screenshot

reinterpreted by composers over the centuries, and in the twenty-first, experimental music mom, New York City–based professor Dafna Naphtali offers up another. Naphtali, together with Kitty Brazelton and drummer Danny Tunick, comprised the group What Is It Like to Be a Bat? Naphtali, who is interviewed in chapter 2, and Brazelton, daughter of famed pediatrician and author of seminal books on infant and child development—including the widely referenced *Touchpoints*—radically reinterpret Italian Baroque composer Pergolesi's 1736 version of "Stabat Mater." First, Naphtali and Brazelton rename it "Stabat.MOM"—and then cut into the musical arrangement and text, disrupting it, diluting it with sounds outside the conventions of mainstream music, thus recasting Mary's suffering story in a way that secularizes and transforms the hymn's liturgical tone, textualizing the figure of the suffering mother with whimsy and irreverence. New York City–based music curator Kathy Supové refers to their collaboration as a "punk digital montage." Indeed, Naphtali and Brazelton update and reshape Pergolesi's "Stabat Mater" almost defiantly. Hasn't Mary suffered enough? Haven't we? In the most positive iterations of mothering, their "cover" or deconstruction is both wildly creative and decidedly resourceful. In our interview, Naphtali relates the creative process of this ultimate mother track:

> I brought in music boxes that you can program. There's Morse code and the sound of pull toys. We rehearsed in the basement and part of the sound is my washing machine: so the piece includes a washing machine sample. We wrote new lyrics that work with these sounds: "The food's on the table getting colder. My face is in the mirror getting older. You're getting older, too, and I'll miss you." Those lines still make me cry. It's both a message to your child and your future self. We created our "Stabat Mater" for a Mother's Day concert and the person who was putting it together told us, "Guys, this is a little dark." But it's the rhythms of mothering: pretty then harsh, pretty then harsh. (Dafna Naphtali in discussion with the author, June 2022)

Supové muses further on the "StaBAT Mom" collaboration in notes promoting her long-running music series, "Music with a View": "This is [. . .] what it's like to be a working mom, [. . .] put through a computer as an isorhythmic/morse code *cantus firmus*, [. . .] some math-rock over it. Into that [. . .] Naphtali's outrageous song fragments about losing one's sense of reality with two active young daughters, weave in Brazelton's 1992 lullaby written when her daughter was three months old with colic" (Dafna Naphtali in an email to the author, June 2022).

In the same interview, Naphtali relates, "No matter where a piece goes, Kitty always ends on a positive note. She's not going to leave it dark, her lyrics: 'I'll be right back, too. Where I was before I had you,' underscore this."

And then Naphtali expresses regret that a piece of such importance had such a small audience, and that it still lives, as of this writing, only on her laptop, "It should have come out. But I've moved on and I'm trying to figure out what to do next, and am feeling connected to the other women I know who have just gotten past this child rearing age [of Stabat Mom]"[2]

In second-wave feminism's groundbreaking interrogation of motherhood under a feminist lens, *Of Woman Born*, writer/poet Adrienne Rich promotes a necessary bifurcation of the role of a mother and her artistic self. She writes: "Once in a while someone used to ask me, 'Don't you ever write poems about your children?' [. . .] For me, poetry was where I lived as no-one's mother, where I existed as myself " (Rich 1976, 31). Almost in implicit response, founding member and lead "mother" of the Pretenders, Chrissie Hynde handily conflates both roles without apology. She adroitly and almost imperceptibly refers to her mother identity in the Pretenders' 1984 hit song, "Middle of

Figure 6.2. Kitty Brazelton with electric bass as part of the band What Is It Like to Be a Bat? performing at the Women's Avant Festival at Lounge Ax in Chicago, October 12, 1997.
Source: Photo by Marc PoKempner, CC BY-SA 4.0

the Road." In her 2019 memoir *Girl to City*, Rigby notes that this song "made a real impression on me, where [Hynde] snapped that she had a kid and was in her thirties. It seemed more punk than the Sex Pistols wanting to destroy. There weren't many female rockers to look up to" (2019, 277). Although aged thirty-two at the time, Hynde's relevant lyrics are pithily delivered: "The babies just come with the scenery," and like Rigby's and Albertine's, autobiographically revealing, "I'm not the cat I used to be / I got a kid, I'm 33" (Hynde 1984). But Hynde doesn't completely and directly explore this rock identity in one of her tracks until "I'm a Mother" from the Pretenders' 1994 album *Last of the Independents*. This is far from the voice of "Stabat Mater," and alludes to Hynde's propensity to downplay the traumatic events she writes about in her 2015 memoir *Reckless*: in other words, if something terrible happened to her, it was no doubt at least partially her fault. "I'm a Mother" proceeds at a clip that leaves no time for regret, only assertion. In a live recording from November 1994, Hynde's opening lyric "I'm a Mother" is delivered as a soaring battle cry that trails off in a quasi-sexual grunt at the end. Motherhood identity is emphatically expressed, in stark contrast to the bereft tone in Ford's opening lyric addressed to her sons, hoping they'll hear it, and listen. In Hynde's "mother cry," she seems to be addressing no one in particular, doesn't seem to care if anyone hears her, believes her, or even wants that particular assertion from her. She's doing the testifying for all.

Sometimes mothers write songs out of an overwhelming need for self-care. And sometimes a mother-fronted band is formed out of that need. Two New York City–based mothers speak to both examples. Rock mom Emily Duff's track "Jesus, Love This Tired Woman" occupies a space very much like "Stabat Mater's." But unlike Naphtali and Brazelton's playful post-modern take, Duff's original, like the lost composer of the thiteenth-century hymn, resides in a faithful space:

> I had been having a lot of health problems at the time. Three neurologists told me I had multiple sclerosis. It turned out I didn't. They told me I was a "burnt out mom" and that I needed to reassess. One of them told me that I had "Mommy Syndrome." It was equivalent to being called "hysterical" in the nineteenth century. I replied, "Are we going 'Charlotte Perkins Gilman' over here?" A major symptom was that I could not sleep. I remember I had been essentially awake for five days. I was at the end of my fucking rope. My kids were both in elementary school. I remember that I couldn't even walk around without crying, because I was fried. When you're a mom, you never want your kids to know you're not feeling well. You have to get everything done, no matter what. I was walking on the edge. And I was also deep into writing songs for my gospel record, *Hallelujah Hello*. While I do go to church, and am a believer, I'm not a crazy, Bible-thumping religious person who prays every day. But I got so close to the edge. I remember very specifically that I got up to take Henry to school.

He was in second grade. I remember walking him to his classroom and as soon as I walked out the door of the school, I started singing the song—essentially writing it in the moment. I felt like I needed a mantra, and it came out as, "Jesus, love this tired woman, Jesus, love this tired woman," and I kept repeating it, and by the time I walked out the door, I started singing the song. I literally sang the entire song off the top of my head. I reached my apartment and grabbed my guitar off the wall and sat down and started playing it. The song was my prayer. I wrote that song as a prayer to help me cope. For my sanity. "No one spends a lifetime running, without falling down dead tired." I was at the end of my rope and was being treated like a hysterical woman, who was fucking out of my mind. The song is a prayer set to melody. And that is how I got through the time of feeling completely out of my head. I used to end every set with this song, taking it into another song off my gospel record because I like to end with a little bit of "church." However, I'm finding that a harder track like "Knuckle Sandwich" is just as much of a prayer—as well as "Razor Blade Smile." Both songs are incredibly punk rock. So I can go from "Jesus" as a plea to "Give you something to cry about," from "Knuckle Sandwich." I go back and forth between the plea—the prayer—to "I'm going to fuck you up," because they both feel like they're both part of the same thing: mommy rage—and strategies to cope with that rage. As a punk, heavily mired in the punk rock of the mid-to-late '70s, I find that I can kick out the jams equally with Jesus or with Johnny Rotten. Both places get me there. Both places are my drug.

All mothers are artists, because we've created. I think a lot about Patti (Smith) and the way she disappeared to be a mother. Everyone said she stopped being an artist, but she didn't stop being an artist. She just tucked into being an artist and went outside of the public sphere, only to come back a thousand times the artist she ever was. Because gestating that creativity in that way brings you to a whole other place. (Emily Duff in discussion with the author, July 2022)

While Duff took up the guitar in girlhood, Dana Schwister, founding member of No Fun, picked up the guitar as a middle-aged mom. Her band, influenced by classic and punk rock—"AC/DC, The Clash, Rolling Stones"—and notably, her son's desire to play guitar, started with herself: one mom teaching herself guitar. Inspired by the punk ethos of the Slits, Schwitzer didn't wait until she had achieved proficiency to perform, and before slowly acquiring band members. Schwister explains:

No Fun started because when my son was seven or eight, he was learning how to play guitar. He liked it for two lessons and then he wanted to quit. I didn't want him to quit, so I got roped in. When my son quit, I continued playing guitar. I was forty years old and it was my first time actually feeling committed to playing. I was playing on his little Yamaha training guitar. The strings are soft. It was hard for me. It was really hard for me to do the chords. I had to actually move my fingers with the other hand. When I had tried to play first at eighteen, I just gave up when it got hard. Older, it was okay that it was harder. I was okay with being slow and taking a long time to learn something. I don't have to be a natural. I was just playing for myself. One summer with a group of families at a lake house, one of the other moms there was annoyed at my son Malachi for something, and said, "I'm never going to feed you again." I thought, I need to write a song about this. Because kids can be so annoying to feed. So I wrote it. Nobody heard it. It was just for myself. I wrote a few other songs. And then I thought, I want to play with somebody. I connected with an old friend of mine, who played drums. We were equally bad. It's very vulnerable to play music. Even talented musicians. I'm not very talented. So it was great to be in a safe, encouraging, non-judgemental space—and just play. We're the same age, same mindset. Doesn't matter if we're good, if we make mistakes. I wrote songs about mothering, songs about aging: "Get Old or Die." First performance was at a Mother's Day event at my friend's mom's loft in Manhattan. I was playing an electric guitar and plugged in. I felt so self-conscious about my guitar playing, I thought I'd just make it very loud and distorted. I had the song "Eyes on the Back of My Head": "I know what you're doing / I know what you said / I've got eyes on the back of my head." I'm talking about a girl who's going after my man, but it's actually inspired by my daughter going after my son to bother him. My kids are always astonished about all of the things I know are happening with them. I have the "Minivan" song. That's a song about the ultimate mom car: a 2007 Honda Odyssey. And that one, too, is a very bluesy riff. The lyrics of "Minivan" are about how I'm getting out of bed super early, because I was actually partying all night. The end turns into a rant about trying to get my kids to shut up and sit down in the van. "I'm not going to say that again."

These songs are meant to be sarcastic and funny. I personally don't think they're angry. I think having the rock 'n' roll layer gets you out of the mothering, which I think is important. We can't be mothers all the time. I might be considered the person who doesn't mother enough. I have a lot of trust that the kids can figure things out on their own and can do things by themselves. I think that's better. My husband criticizes me a lot for this. He worries more about them and wants to do everything for them. My first response is always, "Do it yourself," or "Wait a minute." Attentive mothering doesn't suit my personality and I don't feel like it's helpful to anybody. But mothering is so all encompassing, and all this started when my kids were young. Even if I'm a "hands off" mom, I'm still in it. Your whole world is about these people, who can be very annoying and soul sucking sometimes.

Unfortunately, No Fun is on hiatus. Our guitarist was a kindergarten teacher: really nice, patient, and into what we were doing. He didn't have kids of his own, but he got it. Right now we're looking for a new lead guitarist. I'm not ready to sing and play lead. No Fun is helpful for mothering when I'm actually doing it, even if we're just practicing. It's not really a band if you're not playing. The band name No Fun comes from Iggy Pop, of course. I think we're going to cover "No Fun." A friend of mine told me that one of her childhood friends had a dad, who was a rock and roll freak. For her seventh birthday, he played "No Fun," for all the kids at the party, and it made them all cry. No Fun is also a sarcastic commentary on motherhood. Our band is fun and we make people laugh. But motherhood itself? It really can be no fun. (Dana Schwister in discussion with the author, July 2022)

During her interview, Schwister recited the lyrics for her song "I Won't Be Feeding You Again" to us without musical accompaniment. Clearly satirical, they play with the tropes of mother as strict disciplinarian, the "mean mom," who creates boundaries and enforces them. One can hear strident inflections of Hynde's "I'm a Mother" in these:

> No more pancakes. No more eggs, No more Nutella on your bread.
> No more French fries, no more ketchup, no matter how you cry.
> I won't be feeding you again. I won't be feeding you again.
> No more mac 'n' cheese, no more broccoli trees, no more PBJ, no more Frito Lay.
> I'm sick of the headaches, sick of the heartbreak.
> All these meals thrown in the trash.
> Lasagne and salad, so gross.
> Fish just makes you gag and choke.
> I won't be feeding you again.
> You HATE the yolk? You HATE the yolk?
> Eat your fucking yolk before I shove it down your throat.

Schwister pauses to laugh, and then recites the final lines: "Then the last verse is all the things I'm making without children: anchovies and spicy and sour and salty and strange, and I'm washing it down with an ice-cold brew. That's mothering right there" (Dana Schwister in discussion with the author, July 2022).

When it comes to metal music, it seems almost blaringly obvious that the concept of motherhood would either be engaged within a carnivalesque surrealness or within a horror context—common tropes used within the genre. Metal scholar Amanda DiGorgio has extensively written on motherhood in Finnish heavy metal, citing that mothers are often marginalized and othered, and "rarely depicted subversively" (DiGorgio 2020). The overall conventional norms of heavy metal music demand women be depicted as victims, and yet with the metal moms interviewed in this study, some found ways in which to navigate and create liminal spaces of empowerment.

While not mothers themselves, Mother, a three-piece metal band formed in 2019 hailing from Belgium, engages the topic of motherhood in a unique and rare way by producing content that addresses mental health and motherhood conceptually. Considered members of the "post-metal gaze" genre, Mother's droney musical compositions paired with black metal vocals offer the listener a musical landscape about the liminality of motherhood—a space fertile with the unknown and unventured. When asked why name the band "Mother," Tuur Soete (guitarist and vocalist) provided the following explanation:

> The name "Mother" came from watching *Bates Motel* (I think it was on Netflix at the time) which is a prequel series of *Psycho*. I liked how the relationship between the young Norman Bates and his mother was. It felt like a continuous love and hate relationship in which he very distantly called his mom "mother." So that name was proposed to the band and ultimately stuck. At that time we did not have any lyrics written but we did have a sculpture of a baby that was held by two hands and that we eventually used as a piece of artwork . . . The lyrics (on this album and following albums) tell different stories in the same universe in which a protagonist is guided by a mother figure. It's not always clear though who the mother figure is and if or what she has to gain from her guiding. [sic] (Soete 2021)

This concept of guidance, nurture, and mothering is an overall empowering one, and perhaps a fitting place to end, which harkens back to notions of the primacy of mothering (Rich 1995, 93). It is interesting to see a post-metal band like Mother positioned within a potentially rich area of positive mothering concepts, against the conventions of normal metal music themes. Very few heavy metal bands engage with motherhood as a concept other than to portray the lack of agency of women, or to convey more violent themes of death, gore, abortions, and bad mothering. With the band Mother, we get a completely different take—even the name of the album, *The Loving Care of a Mother for a Child*—is almost unheard of in the genre of post-metal music. Such innovations in typically male-dominated musical subcultures leaves room for more expansive explorations for subversive concepts. Though not comprehensive, there's rife potential here for bands to explore more motherhood adjacent themes.

POST-SCRIPT

Singer/songwriter/mother rocker Amy Rigby was kind enough to dig up and send up a YouTube video of a live performance of her '90s-era all women band, The Shams. Interrupting a set that included two songs about babies, "3 am" and the unrecorded "Little One" that Amy wrote after the birth of her daughter, Hazel, was the following artist/heckler exchange:

> Audience member: "I want to hear about heroin or death."
>
> Rigby: "That's been done before. We wanna sing about babies."
>
> Rigby's band member: "Go buy a Lou Reed record!" (DiMenno 1990)

NOTES

1. The acronym MILF is "Mother I'd like to fuck." How would fellow moms of the PMRC responded to this title?

2. Julie's note: Dafna and I sat in her garden, while she opened her laptop and played "Stabat Mom" for me. The song, which has been presented in this chapter as perhaps angular and difficult, is actually gorgeous and richly layered under Dafna and Kitty's sublime voices, and textualized though Dafna's computer processing. Their harmonies, cut up with the household sounds mentioned in the chapter, dismantled me. Then a phone call. My phone. My daughter on the other end, the one who has been wrestling with herself all summer. "I'm really suffering, Mom," she tells me. The sounds, my daughter, I fail at choking back tears. "I know. I'm suffering with you."

Conclusion

The work of a rock mom book is never done.

How are we ever done with a topic that defines and occupies us so completely? For rock mothering, like all mothering, is an immersive and continuous thing: we're listeners of both music and our children, readers of rock writing and our children's faces and inflections, and when it comes right down to it, both decidedly intensive mothers. At the same time, we attend to ourselves via iterations of heavy music identity participation that has nothing to do with children. We "musick" motherhood. We live it every single day, making adjustments in our lives, from subtle and imperceptible to conspicuous and radical. Likewise, over the course of focused and protracted research for this book, adjustments had to be made on our topic; angles constantly presented themselves. Quite frankly, there is a lot more stuff that should be in this. More mothers we had hoped to talk to—rad rockers we didn't get to write about. Theoretical frameworks we did not get to explore. Already we are thinking ahead to related projects, and thinking back on what this might have been. This chapter is an attempt to address the latter.

Along the way, we have wondered if we've been remiss in not recognizing the complexity of this topic sooner. Did we practice enough care in the process of interviewing the mothers whose experiences are gathered here? As we struggled to define boundaries and definitions, did we cause any pain over the course of these invaluable conversations that we view as the heart of this book? At times, we sent out notes of apology to the mothers of our study, actual and psychic: "I'm sorry for asking you that question and for asking it in that way. We are still learning how to do this."

At book's end, we are still learning how to do this. We wondered if the emphasis we have put on a rock and heavy music lens obscured or inhibited other paths we could have taken. We have hoped our book's content, taken as a whole, highlights that boundaries are porous, and that mothers, like all humans, stagger between and among many identities, sometimes feeling that not one is being fulfilled or realized very well. Whatever that means. One of the things we never questioned was a mother's relationship to music, but often we found ourselves silently wondering in the process: Do you think you're a good mother? Because this is the essential question we ask ourselves frequently. Musicking is easy. Mothering is not. And these mothers at times responded without our asking, obliquely, while making sure other points were tied up. Multitasking. We wondered if we should have revealed more about ourselves. Maybe too late, we got to writer and anthropologist Ruth Behar, who profoundly challenges the historically conventional notions that researchers are structurally and impassively objective in her 1996 seminal text on ethnographic practice *The Vulnerable Observer*. In hindsight, we should have considered her work more of a crucial framework for ours. Behar writes, "Nothing is stranger than this business of humans observing other humans in order to write about them" (1996, 5). She references ethno-psychiatrist George Devereaux, who insisted that "What happens in the observer must be made known" (Behar 1996, 6). Did we do this enough? Did we do it at all? And what was the effect of the labor we asked the real-life vibrant rock 'n' roll mothers to do for this book?

Thinking about a mothering identity, where does one start? When does it start? From one's first experience with their own mothers? Maybe. We didn't ask. Given our lens—this peculiar hard music stance—how much of a future mother's identity was informed by our love of rock and metal that long preceded babies? Does mothering and musicking converge only some of the time? And at others, does it run along parallel tracks, thinking of the mothers in chapter 2 who reported using rock music to escape motherhood, how vital having access to that escape is. We live it. And how much do heavy music identities make the mothering one does more doable, interesting, alive? We should have asked this more. The Slit's guitarist Viv Albertine's quote that ends our rock memoir chapter is just one response to this question. To reference another English "Viv," the first sentence of Vivien Goldman's bustling feminist music history *Revenge of the She Punks*, published in 2019, reminds us how uncool near constant self-conscious questioning can be: "Too obsessive a quest for identity can result in people forgetting who they are" (2019, 17). As Goldman implies, the proto-punk rock women of *She Punks* privilege "being" over "thinking": They lived or are in the process of living these identities. Just as these proto-punk "girls" had no template from which to push off, mothers similarly fend for themselves without role model mothers for guidance and inspiration in every stage of the journey. Like Goldman's array of punk women, mothers of all types largely make it up as they go along. So maybe our book at least partially addresses this "gap," functioning as a handbook of sorts—a "Rock Mom Reader," an introductory text, a primer for an ever-growing group of random, unrelated rock women who don't share a neighborhood playground, but a headspace, an approach to essential imperatives. We reflect on the moment in chapter 3 when Pat Benatar frantically approaches Chrissie Hynde, rock mom to rock mom, begging her for one piece of useful mothering advice, which Chrissie, a bad ass rock 'n' roll powerhouse, does not have. For the famous rock women we studied, those who have adroitly managed a long career and image, motherhood has them overwhelmed, out of advice, speechless.

As we witnessed in this research, as we know implicitly ourselves, rock mothers use heavy music participation as a locus of support—a guitar-driven ersatz group for self-care and self-steeling. In the mode of our heavy music imagination, this has meant bass lines to hold onto, searingly numbing guitar riffages, soothing snare drums at our wombs, sounds as indispensable as a scream, as essential as breathing. Stuff we found out, however: sometimes taking a break from musicking is part and parcel of being a "good mother." Did that break make a difference for their kids? Who knows? We certainly don't. And so when one of the original questions was: Does the freedom of rock dovetail with the restrictions of mothering? We might have to answer: It doesn't.

In the 2022 documentary series *Women Who Rock*, what have always been arbitrary boundaries between music genres are underscored. The conclusion of "Season One Episode Four: Success" touched on the current openness and "hybridity" of popular music, using the example of Gen Z singer / songwriter (and childless!) Billie Eilish, "[who] came up in a post-genre world, and we're seeing what that looks like and what that's going to look like in her music. [. . .] 'Why are the [genres] even separate things?' [she purports] . . . blurring those lines. [. . .]" is seen as a feminist act (Hopper, Women Who Rock, 2022).

At times we referenced the porousness of boundaries and definitions that separate not only music into categories, but also people. As one of our own Gen Z daughters was eager to volunteer, these definitions of gender and gender roles emerged from patriarchy. While music, even what we've called "heavy music," has bloomed into a myriad of subgenres, there have been, it may go without expressing, only two categories shuttling humans along gender lines in white supremacist, colonialist culture: Women / Mother, Man / Father. And when we started this project we worked from this inherited Western binary, perhaps for efficiency's sake, but also out of an implicit acknowledgement that this binary is what the rock moms in our book have had to work with. In 2022, long intact definitions of what a "woman" is, what a "mother" is and what gender is are being radically dismantled, pummeled, interrogated, and reconfigured. It's a construct that we'd like to think that all of our rock 'n' roll mothers here, from those born in the silent generation on, have tried to cut into whether it was co-opting rock styles coded male, like Lita Ford's, Suzi Quatro's, and Chrissie Hynde's respective iterations of "cock rock" that they asserted as early as the '70s. Eschewing "female" rock 'n' roll codes of an "acoustic guitar and piano" that Kathy Valentine refers to, their radical rock moves entailed becoming one of the rocker boys. There has long been room to play with the binary in rock music, shuttling all the way back to its birth in the '50s; a notable and exuberant example is femininely coded legend Little Richard, who English music critic David Hepworth, in his 2017 rock 'n' roll survey *Uncommon People* refers to as "The first rock star" (2017, 1).

We look toward what the present and future holds for mother studies, and if we may assert its natural offshoot: "Rock Mom Studies." And while our particular rock mom study has been almost entirely created from our immersion with Baby Boomer mothers and mothers of Gen X, it is Millennial and Gen Z mothers, who are interrogating these seemingly natural boundaries, asserting a defiant post-gendered stance, a non-binary motherhood. Members of these generational cohorts are now at the age to create their own versions of mothering roles, and their entry into what our book has embodied: a traditional space of rock 'n' roll motherhood—Gen Z might upend the terms. From where we sit, the future of mother studies will be about the decolonization of gender. So maybe the future of "Rock Mom Studies" is embodied in non-binary rock mom LaTisha or Tisha Rico, age twenty-five (as of this writing). Rico are self-described as "Diné (Navajo)." Originally from "Na' Neelzhin (Torreon, New Mexico)," Rico are "indigenous feminist and vegan straight edge," parent of toddler "Bubs," and "front person" of the "Vegan Straight Edge" punk rock band With War, based out of Portland, Oregon (Rico 2018). Rico gave birth to Bubs while With War was on Covid-19–related hiatus, and Bubs is being raised as non-binary with "they/them" pronouns. Rico maintains a personal Instagram account where they feature adorable photos of Bubs in action (@tishxvx. Instagram); this is linked to a band Instagram that features With War in action. In videos posted to With War's account, Rico is not only at the fore, but seemingly often on the floor on the same level as the audience (@withxwar. Instagram). Rico is a dynamic front person, with a powerful voice whose music is part of a long tradition of overtly political punk rock, but crucially advances it from its origins: a Reagan-era white male dominated scene, exemplified in the all-boy hard-core stylings of seminal DC band Minor Threat's "Guilty of Being White." Indeed, a perusal of the With War's social media images reveals its members wearing X's on backs of their hands, same as '80s hardcore kids, like those in Minor Threat and the boys who revered them. Instead, With War's mission, acutely focused on BIPOC issues, seems to be one of radical redress within this genre. With War's Twitter bio—@withxwar—explains their essential ethos: "Anti-colonial" [. . .] "For animals. For humans. For the environment. Liberation for all!" Indigenous rights are promoted in their songs and band merch includes "Land Back" tote bags.

Conclusion

One of the boundaries and definitions we have struggled with has to do with the genre of heavy music. Our decision to write and research within what perhaps has been too limiting of a definition of this term is a central reason our study turned out to be so white. In addition to asking what it might mean to "mother," what does it mean to rock? And who is allowed access to that term? That our book may have functioned as a kind of gatekeeping is troubling. As we want to conclude by looking forward, any "Rock and Mothering Study" should allow for more flexibility in the foundational terms, allowing for a hybridity and fluidity that has come to define both gender and music in our present moment. An adherence to predetermined definitions meant that mothers like Black hardcore rapper Rico Nasty, who has employed and reconfigured classic rock signifiers, and whose music, described as "chaotic" and "in-your-face"—exhibits an array of shifting identities and personas that up the ante on David Bowie.

Even with these glaring omissions, our participant data was abundant. We are still unpacking it. Data collected from our unique online survey provided an unprecedented insight into the demographics of mothers who music hard. Additionally, the rock moms we interviewed "face-to-face"—in person, on Zoom, via our smart phones—were generous with their stories and struggles. In addition to our ethnographic data, we were fortunate to begin this work in a golden era of the rock 'n' roll memoir. While not part of our study, Kristin Hersh's *Seeing Sideways*, her 2020 memoir on music and motherhood, is a standout and should be a key text in further Rock Mother Studies. Hersh's band Throwing Muses defined much of the ethereal, "alternative" feminist-driven popular music of '90s. Her book is an almost hallucinatory mediation of rock mom life on the road, roughing it in a van with a boy brood that eventually grows to four. The only proper names mentioned in the book are those of her four sons, whose respective birth stories she poetically constructs on the page, and in which she defines and redefines notions of her

Figure C.1. Rico Nasty in "OHFR," Official Music Video.
Source: Screenshot

own identity, the way that the stages of motherhood construct that, the ways in which her children's stages help her with those definitions. For Hersh here, the essence of life is motherhood and music. And perhaps it's only right that we end our book with words from hers:

> I wonder if we haven't misunderstood native people who tell us that photographs steal their souls when we call it superstition. The integration of body and soul hits deeper than suspicion of a machine. A baby born into this life *is* life, until we convince it that it must collect the trappings that reflect itself back to us as superficial qualities. [. . .] Without a photographic version of ourselves, we could become our movement, our sound, our words, and our engagement. [. . .] I went back to the guitar. It swung alongside my big stomach so that I could reach it, which was awkward, and I could barely hear the unamplified strings, but it was a way not to look at another angry face or hear another angry voice [. . .] as long as I was playing guitar, that's all I heard.
> This isn't real. Babies and guitars are real. (2022, 151–52)

Lullaby and Goodnight

Rock/Metal Moms We Wanted More of/Didn't Get To: A Playlist Compiled by Joan and Julie

1. Alice Bag, "Turn it Up"
2. Marianne Faithful, "Why D'ya Do It"
3. Rico Nasty, "Rage"
4. Courtney Love, "Uncool"
5. Yoko Ono, "No No No"
6. Tish Rico, WithxWar, "Liberation"
7. Brody Dalle, The Distillers, "Drain the Blood"
8. Tracy Bonham, "Mother, Mother"
9. Moe Tucker, "Hey Mersh"
10. Björk, "Army of Me"
11. Ronnie Spector, "Take Me Home Tonight"
12. Mother, "The Loving Care Of A Mother For A Child"
13. Gospel of the Witches, "Great Mothers"
14. Gospel of the Witches, "Mother"

References

Albertine, Viv. *Clothes, Clothes, Clothes. Music, Music, Music. Boys, Boys, Boys.* New York: St. Martin's, 2014.

Arnett, Jeffrey. *Metalheads: Heavy Metal Music and Adolescent Alienation.* New York: Routledge, 1996.

Arcand, Rob, and Madison Bloom. "7 New Albums You Should Listen to Now: Rico Nasty, Ty Segall, Lil Uzi Vert, and More." *Pitchfork.* Last modified July 22, 2022. https://pitchfork.com/news/7-new-albums-you-should-listen-to-now-rico-nasty-ty-segall-lil-uzi-vert/.

Auerbach, Kari. Interview by author. In person, Phone App Recording. New York City, May 7, 2022.

Bach, Sebastian. *18 and Life on Skid Row.* New York: Dey St., 2016.

Bag, Alice. *Violence Girl: East L.A. Rage to Hollywood Stage, a Chicana Punk Story.* Port Townsend, WA: Feral House, 2011.

Bakhtin, Mikhail. [1936] 1984. *Rabelais and His World.* Translated by H. Iswolsky. Bloomington: Indiana University Press.

Behar, Ruth. *The Vulnerable Observer: Anthropology That Breaks Your Heart.* Boston: Beacon Press, 1996.

Bell, Celeste, and Zoe Howe. *Dayglo: The Poly Styrene Story.* London: Omnibus, 2019.

Bell, Celeste, and Paul Sng, directors. *Poly Styrene: I Am a Cliche.* 2021. Generation Indigo Films. 1 hr., 36 min. https://www.polystyrenefilm.net/.

Benatar, Pat. *Between a Rock and a Heart Place: A Memoir.* New York: William Morrow, 2010.

Benetiz-Eves, Tina. "Tina Turner's Rock & Roll Hall of Fame Induction." *American Songwriter.* Last modified January 2022.

Bracken, Jillian. "Family Music Listening Legacies: A Case Study-based Investigation of the Intergenerational Transmission of Music Listenership Values in Five Families." Dissertation, The University of Western Ontario, 2015. https://ir.lib.uwo.ca/cgi/viewcontent.cgi?article=4276&context=etd.

Bosman, Julie. "Rock Stars of Books: Musicians Big Sales." *New York Times.* Last modified July 8, 2011. https://www.nytimes.com/2011/07/09/books/rock-memoirs-are-popular-with-readers-and-publishers.html#:~:text=%E2%80%9CIt%20appears%20that%20the%20entire,Hagar%20landed%20in%20the%20No.

Brownstein, Carrie. (2009, October 19). Concert Review: Viv Albertine of the Slits. *NPR*. https://www.npr.org/sections/monitormix/2009/10/concert_review_viv_albertine_o.html.

Carlisle, Belinda. *Lips Unsealed: A Memoir*. New York: Crown Archetype, 2010.

Chemaly, Soraya. *Rage Becomes Her*. New York: Simon and Schuster, 2018.

Christopher, Karen. "Extensive Mothering: Employed Mothers' Constructions of the Good Mother." Gender and Society 26, no. 1 (2012): 73–96.

Crawford, Anwen. *Live Through This*. New York: Bloomsbury, 2015.

Cusk, Rachel. *A Life's Work: On Becoming a Mother*. New York: Picador USA, 2021.

Danzig. "Mother." Track 6. *Danzig. Def American*. 1988, Digital.

DiGioia, Amanda. "Nameless, But Not Blameless: Motherhood in Finnish Heavy Metal Music." *Metal Music Studies* 6, no. 2 (2020): 237–55.

DiMenno, Francis and Marguerite. "The Shams (feat. Amy Rigby)." December 1, 1990, YouTube, 45:29. https://www.youtube.com/watch?v=H9uXsljPGUE.

drummy66. Instagram, November 2, 2022. https://www.instagram.com/drummy66/.

Duff, Emily. Interview by author. In person, Phone App Recording. New York City, July 26, 2022.

Duff, Emily. Interview by author. In person, Phone App Recording. New York City, April 6, 2022.

Duff, Emily. Interview by author. In person, Phone App Recording. New York City, April 1, 2019.

Eileraas, Karina. "Witches, Bitches & Fluids: Girl Bands Performing Ugliness as Resistance." *TDR (1988–)* 41, no. 3 (1997): 122–39. https://doi.org/10.2307/1146612.

Felluga, Dino. "Modules on Kristeva: On the Abject." *Introductory Guide to Critical Theory* 31 (2011).

Finn, Natalie. "Stevie Nicks Admits Past Pregnancy with Don Henley's Baby, Talks Cocaine Use and Whether Suicide Ever Crossed Her Mind." *Entertainment Television News*. Last modified September 29, 2014. https://www.eonline.com/news/583768/stevie-nicks-admits-past-pregnancy-with-don-henley-s-baby-talks-cocaine-use-and-whether-suicide-ever-crossed-her-mind.

Ford, Lita. *Living Like a Runaway: A Memoir*. New York: Dey Street, 2016.

Franklin, Dan. *Heavy: How Metal Changes the Way We See the World*. Constable, 2020.

Gaar, Gillian G. *She's a Rebel: The History of Women in Rock & Roll*. New York: Seal Press, 2002.

Gleitsman, Stella. Interview by author. In person, Phone App Recording. New York City, August 12, 2022.

Gleitsman, Zoe. Interview by author. In person, Phone App Recording. New York City, August 12, 2022.

Goldman, Vivien. *Revenge of the She-Punks: A Feminist Music History from Poly Styrene to Pussy Riot*. Austin: University of Texas Press, 2019.

Gordon, Kim. *Girl in a Band: A Memoir*. New York: Dey Street, 2015.

gossett, hattie. "Jazzwomen: They're Mostly Singer and Piano Players. Only a Horn Player or Two. Hardly Any Drummers." In *Rock She Wrote: Women Write About*

Rock, Pop, and Rap, edited by Evelyn McDonnell and Ann Powers, 57–65. Austin: Delta, 1995.

Graham-Bertolini, Alison. *Vigilante Women in Contemporary American Fiction.* New York: Palgrave MacMillan, 2011.

Grácio, Rita. "Daughters of Rock and Moms Who Rock: Rock Music as a Medium for Family Relationships in Portugal." *Revista Crítica de Ciências Sociais* 109 (2016): 83–104.

Grohl, Virgina Hanson. *From Cradle to the Stage: Stories from the Mothers Who Rocked and Raised Rock Stars.* New York: Seal Press, 2017.

Grow, Kory. Dee Snider on PMRC Hearing: "I Was a Public Enemy." *Rolling Stone.* Last modified September 18, 2015. https://www.rollingstone.com/music/music-news/dee-snider-on-pmrc-hearing-i-was-a-public-enemy-71205/.

Hepworth, David. *Uncommon People: The Rise and Fall of the Rock Stars.* London: Bantam Press, 2017.

Hersh, Kristin. *Seeing Sideways: A Memoir of Music and Motherhood.* Austin: University of Texas Press, 2022.

Heti, Sheila. *Motherhood.* New York: Henry Holt, 2018.

Hill, Rosemary Lucy. "Pleasure in Metal: What Women Fans Like About Hard Rock and Metal Music." In *Heavy Metal Generations*, pp. 117–127. Boston: Brill, 2012.

Hoad, Catherine. "'Scream bloody gore'-the abject body and posthuman possibilities in death metal." *NEO: Journal for Higher Degree Research in the Social Sciences and Humanities* 5 (2012): 1–14.

Hopper, Jessica. Interview by author. Zoom. Chicago/New York City, July 28, 2022.

Jamieson, Christine. *Powers of Horror: An Essay on Abjection: Julia Kristeva's Contribution to the Topic of Sexual Differentiation.* Saint Paul University, 1990.

Jones, Grace. *I'll Never Write My Memoirs.* New York: Gallery Books, 2015.

Kahn-Harris, Keith. *Extreme Metal: Music and Culture on the Edge.* Oxford: Berg, 2007.

Kelly, K. (2020, November 12). "Inside Heavy Metal's Battle Against White Supremacy." *Esquire.* Retrieved from https://www.esquire.com/entertainment/music/a34633291/heavy-metal-nazi-anti-fascist-movement/.

Kelly, Tamara (2020, March 17). "Myrkur Is Reclaiming Her Scandinavian Roots and Blossoming into Motherhood." *The Line of Best Fit.* Retrieved from https://www.thelineofbestfit.com/features/interviews/myrkur-blossoming-into-motherhood.

Kitteringham, Sarah. "Extreme Conditions Demand Extreme Responses: The Treatment of Women in Black Metal, Death Metal, Doom Metal, and Grindcore." Master's thesis, Graduate Studies, 2014.

Kristeva, Julia. *Powers of Horror: An Essay in Abjection.* Translated by Leon Roudiez. New York: Columbia University Press, 1982.

Lavare, Daryl. Interview by author. In person, Phone App Recording. New York City, June 13, 2022.

Mahon, Maureen. *Black Diamond Queens: African American Women and Rock and Roll.* Durham, NC: Duke University Press, 2020.

Maloney, Nancy. Interview by author. In person, Phone App Recording. New York City, July 25, 2022.

McClary, Susan. *Feminine Endings: Music, Gender, and Sexuality*. University of Minnesota Press, 2002.

"A Metal Mother's Day Chat with Lita Ford + 'Mother' Track Premiere." *Decibel*. Last modified May 11, 2012.

Mitchell, Joni, "Free Man in Paris," Track 3 on Court and Spark, Asylum, 1974, lp album.

Moan Elisa. Interview by author. In person, Phone App Recording. New York City, March 24, 2022.

Naphtali, Dafna. Interview by author. In person, Phone App Recording. New York City, June 29, 2022.

Osbourne, Ozzy. "Mama, I'm Coming Home." Track 3. *No More Tears*. Epic, 1992.

Pearson, Tonya. *Why Marianne Faithfull Matters*. Austin: University of Texas Press, 2021.

Perl, Puma. Interview by author. Email. New York City, April 3, 2019.

Phair, Liz. "Little Digger." Track 7 on Liz Phair. Capitol Records, Spotify, 2003.

Phillipov, Michelle. *Death Metal and Music Criticism: Analysis at the Limits*. Lanham, MD: Lexington Books, 2012.

Poneman, Jonathan. "Our December 1992 Cover Story: 'Family Values.'" *Spin*. Last modified December 12, 2017. https://www.spin.com/featured/our-december-1992-cover-story-family-values/.

Purcell, Natalie J. *Death Metal Music: The Passion and Politics of a Subculture*. Jefferson, NC: McFarland, 2003.

Quatro, Suzi. *Unzipped*. London: Hodder, 2008.

Reynolds, Simon, and Joy Press. *The Sex Revolts: Gender, Rebellion and Rock 'n' Roll*. Cambridge: Harvard University Press, 1995.

Rich, Adrienne. *Of Woman Born*. New York: W. W. Norton, 1976.

Rich, Adrienne. *Of Woman Born: Motherhood as Experience and Institution*. New York: W. W. Norton & Company, 1995.

Riches, Gabrielle. "Embracing the Chaos: Mosh Pits, Extreme Metal Music and Liminality." *Journal for Cultural Research* 15, no. 3 (2011): 315–32.

Rico, La Tisha. Interview with Tuck Woodstock. *Gender Reveal*. Podcast audio. March 5, 2018.

Rigby, Amy. *Girl to City: A Memoir*. Catskill, NY: Southern Domestic, 2019.

Ritlop, Tina. "'You Scream like a Girl': Growling and Screaming Female Voices in Metal Music." In *Words, Music and Gender*, edited by Michelle Gadpaille and Victor Kennedy, 149–57. Newcastle Upon Tyne, England: Cambridge Scholars, 2020.

Robinson, Lisa. *Nobody Ever Asked Me About the Girls: Women, Music and Fame*. New York: Henry Holt, 2020.

Rose, L. Ross, and J. Hartmann (Eds.), *Music of Motherhood: History, Healing, and Activism* (pp. 32–50). Ontario, Canada: Demeter Press, 2017.

Rose, M. Joy. *Music of Motherhood: History, Healing, Activism*. Ontario, Cananda: Demeter Press, 2017.

Ross, Cynthia. Interview by author. Phone Call. New York City, April 2019.

Russo, Stacy. *We Were Going to Change the World: Interviews with Women From the 1970s and 1980s Southern California Punk Rock Scene*. Solana Beach, CA: Santa Monica Press, 2017.

Savage, Sally, and Clare Hall. "Thinking About and Beyond the Cultural Contradictions of Motherhood through Musical Mothering." In *Music of Motherhood: History, Healing, and Activism*, edited by M. J. Rose, Lynda Ross, and Jennifer Hartmann, 32–50. Ontario, Canada: Demeter Press, 2017.

Schemel, Patty. Hit *So Hard: A Memoir*. Boston: Da Capo Press, 2017.

Schonfeld, Zach. "Parental Advisory Forever: An Oral History of the PMRC." *Newsweek*. Last modified September 19, 2015. https://www.newsweek.com/2015/10/09/oral-history-tipper-gores-war-explicit-rock-lyrics-dee-snider-373103.html.

Schwister, Dana. Interview by author. In person, Phone App Recording. New York City, July 25, 2022.

Sembuya, Rita. "Mother or Nothing: The Agony of Infertility." Bull World Health Organ 2010; 88: 881–82. Retrieved from https://www.scielosp.org/article/ssm/content/raw/?resource_ssm_path=/media/assets/bwho/v88n12/v88n12a05.pdf.

Shadrack, Jasmine Hazel. "Femme-liminale: Corporeal Performativity in Death Metal." In *Metal and Marginalisation Conference: Gender, Race, Class and Other Implications for Hard Rock and Metal*. 2014.

Sheffield, Rob. "The 50 Greatest Rock Memoirs of All Time." *Rolling Stone*. Last modified December 19, 2020. https://www.rollingstone.com/music/music-lists/books-greatest-rock-memoirs-of-all-time-161198/steven-tyler-does-the-noise-in-my-head-bother-you-2011-36147/.

Simpson, Rose. *Muse, Odalisque, Handmaiden: A Girl's Life in The Incredible String Band*. London: Strange Attractor Press, 2020.

Small, Christopher. *Musicking: The Meanings of Performing and Listening*. Hanover: University Press of New England, 1990.

Smith, Patti. *Just Kids*. New York: Ecco, 2010.

Soete, Tuur. Interview by author. Email. California, August 16, 2022.

Staff, Communication and Marketing. "Annenberg Inclusion Initiative's Annual Report on Popular Music Reveals Little Progress for Women." *USC Annenberg School for Communication and Journalism*, March 8, 2021. https://annenberg.usc.edu/news/research-and-impact/annenberg-inclusion-initiatives-annual-report-popular-music-reveals-little.

Sundaramurthy, Mallika. Interview by author. Email. New York City, March 3, 2021.

The Irish Times. Last modified July 31, 2019. https://www.irishtimes.com/culture/art-and-design/visual-art/kim-gordon-i-never-think-of-myself-as-famous-i-m-barely-famous-1.3969888.

The Pretenders. 1984. "Middle of the Road." Track 1 on *Learning to Crawl*. Rhino—Warner Records, Spotify.

Three Dog Night. "Mama Told Me Not to Come." Track 7. *It Ain't Easy*. Dunhill, 1970.

Tipton, Gemma. "Kim Gordon: 'I Never Think of Myself as Famous—I'm Barely Famous.'" *The Irish Times*. Last modified July 31, 2019. https://www.irishtimes.com/culture/art-and-design/visual-art/kim-gordon-i-never-think-of-myself-as-famous-i-m-barely-famous-1.3969888.

Tishxvx. Instagram, August 14, 2022. https://www.instagram.com/tishxvx/.

Turner, Tina. *My Love Story.* New York: Atria Books, 2018.

Unruly, Julie. Interview by author. In person, Phone App Recording. New York City, January 26, 2022.

Valentine, Kathy. *All I Ever Wanted: A Rock 'n' Roll Memoir.* Austin: University of Texas Press, 2020.

Vasan, Sonia. "'Den Mothers' and 'Band Whores': Gender, Sex and Power in the Death Metal Scene." In *Heavy Fundametalisms: Music, Metal and Politics*, pp. 67–77. Brill, 2010.

Vozick-Levinson, Simon. "Say Hello to the Next Great New York Rock Band." *Rolling Stone.* Last modified November 2, 2022. https://www.rollingstone.com/music/music-features/hello-mary-new-york-band-1234607414/.

Walser, Robert. *Running with the Devil: Power, Gender, and Madness in Heavy Metal Music.* Middletown, CT: Wesleyan University Press, 1993.

Waters, Daniel. "'Better Than Clearasil': How X-ray Spex Allowed me to See Past My Germ-filled Adolescence." In *Here She Comes Now: Women in Music Who Changed Our Lives*, edited by Jeff Gordinier and Marc Weingarten, 153–61. Los Angeles: Barnacle, 2015.

Weinstein, Deena. *Heavy Metal: The Music and Its Culture.* Boston: Da Capo Press, 1991.

Weinstein, Deena. *Heavy Metal: The Music and Its Culture*, revised edition. Boston: Da Capo Press, 2000.

Willis, Ellen. *Out of the Vinyl Deeps: Ellen Willis on Rock Music.* Minneapolis: University of Minnesota Press, 2011.

Whizbanger, Sara. Interview by author. In person, Phone App Recording. Portland, OR, July 28, 2021.

withxwar. Instagram, August 14, 2022, https://www.instagram.com/withxwar/.

X-Ray Spex. 1978. "Identity." Track 2 on Germ Free Adolescents. EMI, Spotify.

Zadroga, Mary. Interview by author. In person, Phone App Recording. New York City, March 21, 2022.

Zeitz, J. "Rejecting the Center: Radical Grassroots Politics in the 1970s—Second-Wave Feminism as a Case Study." *Journal of Contemporary History* 43, no. 4 (2008): 673–88. http://www.jstor.org/stable/40543229.

Index

18 and Life on Skid Row (Bach), 56–57

abjection, 13–14
abortion, 28, 40, 59, 90–91
activism, 40
agency: body and, 15; self-silencing and lack of, 80–81; sexual, 26; vigilante motherhood and, 80–83; voice and, 80–82
AIDS/HIV, 59
Albertine, Viv, 59–62, 77, 87, 90, 110; on alienation, 72–73; lyrics of, 97–99
alienation, 13–14, 70–74
All I Ever Wanted (Valentine), 59
anger, 79–83
anxiety, 65, 82–83
Armageddon, Helixx C., 48–54
Auerbach, Kari, 30–31

Bach, Sebastian, 56–57
Bag, Alice, 59
Bakhtin, Mikhail, x
balance: as lie, 45; self-care and, 17
Bean, Frances, xx–xxi
Behar, Ruth, 110
Bell, Celeste, 9, 85–87
Benatar, Pat, 110–11; on childcare, 71, 73; *Between a Heart and a Rock Place* by, 58, 60; pregnancy of, 65, 66–67
Between a Heart and a Rock Place (Benatar), 58, 60
Beyonce, 44
'B' Girls, ix, 16–17
bikers, 31
BIPOC women, xiv–xv, 5, 61, 74–75, 112
Black musicians, 5, 61, 74–75
body: abject, 13–14; agency and, 15; freedom and, 21; image, 1–2; motherhood and, 32–33, 70–71; pregnancy and, 13–15, 42, 90–91
bonding, 87–94
Brazelton, Kitty, 101, *102,* 108n2
breastfeeding, xvi, 42–43, 70
Brigham Young University, xviii–xix
Brown, Bobbie, 60
Brownstein, Carrie, 75–76
Brunn, Amalie, 82
Bush, Kate, 5

capitalism, 85
career: feminism and, 62–63; gender and, 29, 62; motherhood and, 29–31, 41–46, 52–54, 56–77; music industry and, 60; pregnancy and, 64–70; of rock moms, 56–77

Carlisle, Belinda, 60, 64, 69, 70
Chemaly, Soraya, 15, 79–80
Cher, 62
childbirth, ix, 16, 31; identity after, 28, 74; pregnancy and, 13, 22, 24, 32, 68–71; sex after, 70; vulnerabilities and strength during, 14
childcare: cost of, 30; gender and, 22–23, 70–71; rock moms and, 70–75; self-care and, 74; touring and, 70–75, 83
childless women, 9–10, 23, 56
children: daughters, of rock moms, xxi–xxii, 2, 75, 85–94; life meaning and, 28, 30, 31; music and, 24–25, 85, 88–90; musicking, x, 87–90; not talking about, 55–58; not wanting to have, 12, 20, 24, 28, 30; supporting passions of, 25; wellbeing of, 75–77, 86–87
Chrysalis, 63
Clothes Music Boys (Albertine), 60
clothing, 22, 31–32, 40, 50; pregnancy and, 66–67
Cobain, Kurt, xx–xxi
costumes, 32
Crawford, Anwen, xxi
creativity, 17, 31, 33, 86, 92; pregnancy and, 67–68
culture, xvii–xviii, 46, 82–83; ethnicity and, xii–xiii; norms and, 11–12
Cusk, Rachel, xx

dads, 29, 38, 44, 58, 70
data, 6–7, *7,* 61–62, 113
dating, 18–19
daughters: mother-daughter bonding and, 87–94; musicking and, 87–90; of rock moms, xxi–xxii, 2, 75, 85–94
"Daughters of Rock and Moms Who Rock" (Grácio), 2, 87–89
Davis, Christy, 27–28, 92–94, *93*
death metal. *See* extreme metal music
deejays, 27
demographic data, 6–7, *7,* 61–62

Des Barres, Pamela, 60
design, 30–31
Devereaux, George, 110
DiGorgio, Amanda, 106
DiMenno, Francis and Marguerite, 108
Dirty Rocker Boys (Brown), 60
divorce, 70, 79–80
drugs, 34, 57, 59, 64, 69
Duff, Emily, *20,* 20–22, 103–4

economy, 32, 85
Eileraas, Karen, 81
Elisa, Moan, 31–33, *88*
Elliott-Said, Marianne Joan, 85–86
Embree, Dana Marie, 46–48
EMM. *See* extreme metal music
empowerment, 80–83
ethics, 26–27
ethnicity, xxii; BIPOC women and, xiv–xv, 5, 61, 112; culture and, xii–xiii; fetishizing, xiv–xv
extreme metal music (EMM), xiii–xiv, 2, 14. *See also* metal

Faithfull, Marianne, xvi
family planning, 65
fans, 30, 36, 40–41
fears, 13–14
Feminine Endings (McClary), 1–2
The Feminine Mystique (Friedan), 62
femininity, 2
feminism, xvii–xviii, 17, 28; career and, 62–63; ethics and, 26–27; men and, 26; in metal, 26–27; punk, 40–41; race and, 26, 62; Riot Grrrls and, 25–26; second-wave white, 62–63, 102–3; stripping and, 26–27
fertility, 64, 67–68, 82–83, 98–99
finances, 29–30, 62, 68–69
Ford, Lita, 60, *100*; on alienation, 73–74; lyrics of, 99–100; pregnancy of, 64–65, 69
freedom, 21, 36, 92
free-range parenting, xvii
Friedan, Betty, 62

Gallo, Vincent, 72
gender, x, 3–4; career and, 29, 62; childcare and, 22–23, 70–71; culture and roles of, 82–83; finances and, 62; fluidity, 25; identity and, 72; language and, 81–82; metal and, xiii–xv, 2, 27; in music industry, 1–2; parenting and, 11–12, 37, 91–92; pregnancy and, 17; stage performance and, 27
generational differences, xvii–xix, 93, 111–12
Girl in a Band (Gordon), 60–61, 62
Girl to City (Rigby), 60–63, 65–66, 103
Gleitsman, Zoe, 90–91
Goldman, Vivien, 110
Gordon, Kim, 56–57, 60–61, 62; on childcare, 70–72; on identity, 72; pregnancy of, 65
Goude, Jean Paul, 69–70
Grácio, Rita, 2, 87–89
Gray, Macy, 45
grief, xv, 75, 89
Griffith, Nancy, 89
Grohl, Dave, 5–6
Grohl, Virginia Hanlon, 5–6
groupies, 60
Guerrilla Girls, 23
guilt, 33, 72–75

Hall, Clare, 55
"having it all," 63; as lie, 16–17, 21, 29–30, 45, 52–53, 72–73; multitasking and, 72–75, 110
Hays, Sharon, 76
heavy music, 3–4, 5, 13, 96–107, 113
helicopter parenting, 25
Hersh, Kristin, 60, 113–14
Heti, Sheila, 9–10
High & Tight, 17–19
Hill, Lauryn, 91
hip hop, 50, 113
Hit So Hard (Schemel), 59
HIV/AIDS, 59
Hoad, Catherine, 13–14

Hockley, Tanya, 37–39
homophobia, 26
honesty, 25
Hopper, Jessica, 39–46, 60
housing, 47–48
hymns, 100–101
Hynde, Chrissie, 5, 59, 73, 103, 110–11

ideals, xvii, 9–16
identity: after childbirth, 28, 74; gender and, 72; motherhood and, xx–xxi, 11–16, 25, 28, 33, 48, 52–54, 91, 102–3, 109–14; music, 24–26, 33–34, 40, 47, 49–51, 112–14; pregnancy and, 66–67; religion and, xvi–xix; rock moms and, 66–67, 72–74, 86, 109–14; rock star, xxi; self and, 11–12, 74; women and, xviii–xix, 9–10
I'll Never Write My Memoirs (Jones, G.), 60–61
image, 1–2, 57, 70, 75
I'm with the Band (Des Barres), 60
insecurity, 25
intensive mothering, 76
interviews: one-on-one interview participants, 7; qualitative, 9–11, 56. *See also specific topics; specific women*

Jocson-Singh, Joan, *xi*, 11; on embodying the visceral, 13–15; insights of, 79–83; Joan's story, x–xv
Jones, Grace, 60–61, *61*, 64; pregnancy of, 69–70
Jones, Rickie Lee, 45
Joplin, Janis, 24
Just Kids (Smith), 57, 59

Karyn Crisis, xii, xiii
Kristeva, Julia, 13–14

Lamott, Anne, 63
language, 81–82
LaVare, Darryl, 35–37

LGBTQIA community, 62, 89, 91–92
lies: balance as, 45; on "having it all," 16–17, 21, 29–30, 45, 52–53, 72–73; on motherhood, 33
life meaning, 28, 30, 31
A Life's Work (Cusk), xx
Lips Unsealed (Carlisle), 60
Living like a Runaway (Ford), 60
loudness, 35
Love, Courtney, xx–xxi

Mahon, Maureen, 5
Maloney, Nancy, 33–34
marginalization, xx, xxii, 14, 17, 62–63, 106
marriage: divorce and, 70, 79–80; motherhood and, xix, 45–46, 97; parenting and, 70; religion and, xvii; same-sex, 91–92
masculinity, 2, 27
McClary, Susan, 1–2
men: dads, 29, 38, 44, 58, 70; feminism and, 26; masculinity and, 27
mental health: anxiety and, 65, 82–83; post-partum depression and, 34; PTSD and, 25, 41, 54; rock moms and, 65, 75–76, 86–87, 103–4. *See also* trauma
metal, xii, 50–51; EMM, xiii–xiv, 2; feminism in, 26–27; gender and, xiii–xv, 2, 27; rock moms and, 82, 89, 95–108; vigilante motherhood and, 82; whiteness of, 4–5
Metallica, xiii
MILF acronym, 19, 98, 108n1
miscarriage, 68
Mitchell, Joni, 57
Mormon families, xvi–xix
mosh pit, 36
Mother (band), 106–7
mother-child relationships, 11–12, 75–77, 85–94
mother-daughter bonding, 87–94
mother framing: framework for, 1–4; methodologies for, 1–4, 5–7, 7; participants, from one-on-one interviews, 7; rock and metal's whiteness relating to, 4–5; women, heavy music, and, 3–4, 5
motherhood: as antithetical to rock music, 43–44; body and, 32–33, 70–71; career and, 29–31, 41–46, 52–54, 56–77; embodying the visceral in, 13–14; extremes of, x; fears, 13–14; ideals and, xvii, 9–16; identity and, xx–xxi, 11–16, 25, 28, 33, 48, 52–54, 91, 102–3, 109–14; image and, 57, 70, 75; Joan's story of, x–xv; Julie's story of, xvi–xxii; lies on, 33; marginalization of, xx, xxii; marriage and, xix, 45–46, 97; meaning and definitions of, ix–x, 11–13; musicking and, x, 10, 72–73, 76–77, 109–10; norms, 11–12; patriarchy and, 12–13; religion and, xvi–xix; responsibilities of, 16, 21, 47–48, 52–53; self and, 11–13, 70–75; self-expression and, xix–xxi; single, 16, 18–19, 44, 52; spiritual nature of, 45–46; suffering and, 82–83; "trouble" in, 9–10; vigilante, 79–83; vulnerability and, 4–15, 75–76; writing and lyrics on, 95–108. *See also specific topics*
Motherhood (Heti), 9–10
mother-performers, 81–82. *See also* stage performance
MTV News, 44–45
multitasking, 72–75, 110
music: children and, 24–25, 85, 88–90; festivals, xxi; heavy, 3–4, 5, 13, 96–107, 113; identity, 24–26, 33–34, 40, 47, 49–51, 112–14; parenting and, 2–3, 12, 95–96, 106; as self-care, 6, 18–19, 27, 36–37; streaming, 51–52. *See also* metal; popular music; rock music
music industry: appearances and, 43; career and, 60; gender in, 1–2; pregnancy in, 21; PTSD and, 41;

record labels, 50–52, 58, 60, 63; representation in, 1–2; sexism in, xiv–xv, xx, 21–22, 41, 57, 63
music journalism, 41–42
musicking, xxii; children, x, 87–90; daughters and, 87–90; lived experience of, 5–6; as meaning-making, x; motherhood and, x, 10, 72–73, 76–77, 109–10; rock moms and, 55–56, 60, 72–73, 76–77
My Love Story (Turner), 60–61

Naphtali, Dafna, 101–2, 108n2
Napster, 51
narratives, xv; of rock moms, xxii, 57–58
Nashville Pussy, 37–39, 56
neoliberalism, 85
norms, 11–12
nostalgia, 89

Of Woman Born (Rich), 102–3
Oldham, Andrew Loog, xvi
one-on-one interview participants, 7
Operating Instructions (Lamott), 63
The Osmond Brothers, xvii

parenting, 80; free-range, xvii; gender and, 11–12, 37, 91–92; helicopter, 25; marriage and, 70; mother-child relationships and, 11–12, 75–77, 85–94; music and, 2–3, 12, 95–96, 106
Parents Music Resource Center (PMRC), 95–96
Paris, Jesse, 85
patriarchy, 12–13
Pearson, Tanya, xvi
Perl, Puma, *3,* 22–23
Phair, Liz, 96
phallic drive, xxi
PMRC. *See* Parents Music Resource Center
Poly Styrene (documentary), 85–87
Poneman, Jonathan, xx–xxi

popular music, xx–xxi, 1, 5, 25, 44, 57, 111, 113
post-partum depression, 34
post-traumatic stress disorder (PTSD), 25, 41, 54
pregnancy, xiv; abject body and, 13–14; abortion and, 28, 40, 59, 90–91; body and, 13–15, 42, 90–91; career and, 64–70; childbirth and, 13, 22, 24, 32, 68–71; clothing and, 66–67; complications, 64, 69; creativity and, 67–68; fertility and, 64, 67–68, 82–83, 98–99; gender and, 17; identity and, 66–67; miscarriage and, 68; in music industry, 21; risks, 13; rock moms and, 64–70, 91; self-care during, 64–66, 68–69; shame and, 63, 64; single motherhood and, 47–48; stage performance during, 21, 22, 28–29, 51, 66–67; touring and, 51, 65–69; visceral experience of, 66–67
Presley, Elvis, 5
Pretenders, 59
privilege, 74–75
PTSD. *See* post-traumatic stress disorder
punk feminism, 40–41
punk rock, xii, 9, 19, 40

Quatro, Suzi, 59, 60–61, 64; on childcare, 71–72; pregnancy of, 66–68, 70

race, xxii, 85–86; BIPOC women and, xiv–xv, 5, 61, 74–75, 112; feminism and, 26, 62; whiteness and, 4–5, 112
racism, 35–36, 74
rage, 79–83
rap, 50, 113
Reckless (Hynde), 59
recording studios, 21–22
record labels, 50–52, 58, 60, 63
religion, xvi–xix, 100–101
representation, 1–2, 4–5
repressive mothering, 95–96

responsibility, 16, 21, 47–48, 52–53
Revenge of the She Punks (Goldman), 110
Rich, Adrienne, 102–3
Richards, Keith, 57
Rico, Tisha, 112
Rico Nasty, 113, *113*
Rigby, Amy, 107–8; on childcare, 71, 73, 74; *Girl to City* by, 60–63, 65–66, 103; on guilt, 73; lyrics of, 96–97; pregnancy of, 65–67
Rihanna, 91
Riot Grrrls, 25–26
rock moms: alienation of, 70–74; career of, 56–77; childcare and, 70–75; child wellbeing and, 75–77; daughters of, xxi–xxii, 2, 75, 85–94; identity and, 66–67, 72–74, 86, 109–14; image of, 75; memoirs, 55–77; mental health and, 65, 75–76, 86–87, 103–4; metal and, 82, 89, 95–108; mothering narratives of, xxii; multitasking by, 72–75, 110; musicking and, 55–56, 60, 72–73, 76–77; narratives of, xxii, 57–58; "no talking about the baby" for, 55–58; pregnancy and, 64–70, 91; qualitative interviews with, 9–11; vignettes, 11–54; writing motherhood and lyrics of, 95–108
rock music: motherhood as antithetical to, 43–44; phallic drive in, xxi; punk rock, xii, 9, 19, 40; rock star identity and, xxi; sexism in, xx; types of, xii–xiii; whiteness of, 4–5; women, heavy music, and, 3–4, 5, 13, 96–107, 113
Rosenfeld, Maria, 29
Ross, Cynthia, ix, 16–17, *18*

same-sex marriage, 91–92
satire, 105–6
Savage, Sally, 55
Schemel, Patty, 59
Schwister, Dana, 104–6
Scream Bloody Gore (Hoad), 13
second-wave white feminism, 62–63, 102–3
Seeing Sideways (Hersh), 60, 113–14
self: identity and, 11–12, 74; motherhood and, 11–13, 70–75; as selflessness, 11–13; silencing of, 74–75, 79–83
self-care: anger and, 79–80; balance and, 17; childcare and, 74; music as, 6, 18–19, 27, 36–37; need for, 103–4; during pregnancy, 64–66, 68–69; responsibility and, 16–17; suffering and, 82–83; vigilante motherhood and, 79–83
self-esteem, 17–19, 25
self-expression, xix–xxi; creativity and, 17, 31, 33, 67–68, 86, 92
Sembuya, Rita, 82–83
sex: after childbirth, 70; sexual agency and, 26
sexism: internalization of, 79; in music industry, xiv–xv, xx, 21–22, 41, 57, 63; in rock music, xx; stage performance and, 21, 22, 41
shame, 63, 64, 90
The Shams, 107–8
Sheer Frost Orchestra, 29
Sheffield, Rob, 58
Simpson, Rose, 75–76
single motherhood, 16, 18–19, 44, 52; pregnancy and, 47–48
The Slits, 61–62, 97–98
Small, Christopher, x, 87–89
Smith, Patti, 5, 22–23, 45–46, 57, 59–60, 72; daughter of, 85
Snare Drum at My Womb (Davis), 92–93
social constraints, 17
social order, 9–10
social pressures, 11–12
Soete, Tuur, 107
songwriting, 95–108
Sonic Youth, 56–57, 62, 65, 71
spiritual nature of motherhood, 45–46

stage performance, 69, 81–82; gender and, 27; during pregnancy, 21, 22, 28–29, 51, 66–67; sexism and, 21, 22, 41
streaming music, 51–52
stripping, 26–27
Styrene, Poly, 9, 85–87
success, 55–56
suffering, 75, 82–83, 97–101
suicide, 75
Sundaramurthy, Mallika, 11–12, 14–15, 89–90
Suys, Henk and Ruyter, 37–39

Take Another Little Piece of My Heart (Des Barres), 60
Thornton, Big Mama, 5
thrifting, 49–50
touring, 12, 28–30, 35, 39–45, 56; childcare and, 70–75, 83; pregnancy and, 51, 65–69
transgressive mothering, 13
trauma, 17, 24, 68, 75; PTSD and, 25, 41, 54
"trouble," 9–10
Tuckey, Len, 68–69
Tunick, Danny, 101
Turley, Julie, *xvi*, 11; insights of, 55–77; Julie's story, xvi–xxii
Turner, Tina, 60–61, 62, 63–64; on childcare, 74–77; on multitasking, 74–75; pregnancy of, 67, 68–69

ugliness, 81–82
Unruly, Julie, *15*, 17–19
UnZipped (Quatro), 60–61, 67–68

Valentine, Kathy, 59–60
vigilante motherhood, 79–83
violence, 25–26, 79
Violence Girl (Bag), 59
Virgin Mary, 100–101
visibility, 43
voice, 80–82. *See also* agency
vulnerability: during childbirth, 14–15; motherhood and, 4–15, 75–76
The Vulnerable Observer (Behar), 110

Warhol, Andy, 64
wealth, 29
whiteness, 4–5, 112
white supremacy, 4–5
Whizbanger, Sara, 23–27
Why Marianne Faithfull Matters (Pearson), xvi
Willis, Ellen, xx–xxi
women: BIPOC, xiv–xv, 5, 61, 74–75, 112; Black musicians, 5, 61, 74–75; childless, 9–10, 23, 56; heavy music and, 3–4, 5, 13, 96–107, 113; identity and, xviii–xix, 9–10; social order and, 9–10; violence against, 25–26, 79. *See also specific topics*
"Women's Music" (Willis), xxi
Women Who Rock (documentary series), 39–40, 45, 111
working hours, 42
working mothers, 56–57, 70, 76. *See also specific topics*

Zadroga, Mary, 34–35

About the Authors

Julie Turley, MFA/MLS, is an assistant professor and open education librarian at Kingsborough Community College/City University of New York in Brooklyn. She is also a fiction writer, whose work has appeared in *North American Review, Quarterly West*, and *Western Humanities Review*, among other journals. She has published and presented on wide-ranging topics, including OERs and open pedagogy, college library pandemic-era Instagram posting, addiction and recovery in rock 'n' roll memoirs, Mötley Crüe, and most recently, on the involvement and identity of mothers who participate in rock and heavy metal music, on which, with Joan Jocson-Singh, she presented at the 2019 Modern Heavy Metal Conference in Helsinki, Finland.

Joan Jocson-Singh, MLS/MA, is the Library Director at the Lucas Museum of Narrative Art, Los Angeles, California. She has previously worked as Institute Librarian at the California Institute of the Arts (CalArts) and as Head of Technical Services at Lehman College, Bronx, New York. She has presented her thesis work, "Individual Thought Patterns: Women in NY's Extreme Metal Music Scene" at the 2014 Metal and Cultural Impact (MACI) conference in Dayton, Ohio, the Northeast Regional Popular Culture Association (PCA) conference in Providence, Rhode Island, in 2014, and the 2016 Experience Museum Project (EMP) conference in Seattle, Washington. Joan's research interests include IDEA and Zines in Librarianship, Women and Motherhood Studies, Sexuality Studies and Ethnomusicology. She is the author of the 2019 article, "Vigilante Feminism as a Form of Musical Protest in Extreme Metal Music," published by Intellect in *Metal Music Studies*.

www.ingramcontent.com/pod-product-compliance
Lightning Source LLC
Chambersburg PA
CBHW052051300426
44117CB00012B/2070